Prayer

Prayer

A Christian Companion

Susan Hibbins

Copyright © Trustees for Methodist Church Purposes, 2006
Cover picture photo: © LiquidLibrary

British Library Cataloguing in Publication data

A catalogue record for this book is available
from the British Library

ISBN 1-85852-317-6
978-1-85852-317-0

First published by Inspire
4 John Wesley Road
Werrington
Peterborough PE4 6ZP

Printed and bound in Great Britain by
Stanley L. Hunt (Printers) Ltd, Rushden

Contents

Foreword

Every day on my drive to and from work I pass a particular tree. It reminds me of the trees that are sometimes pictured in children's story books, which are depicted with human shapes; or the fabled Ents in Tolkien's *The Lord of the Rings*. It has two branches which resemble arms on either side of it, and to my perhaps over-active imagination the tree always seems to be holding up its 'arms' in prayer: in the summer, when the sun is shining and nature is full of abundance, its arms are raised to worship and thank God for all that is good in life; in the winter, when the wind has stripped away its leaves and it endures the worst weather, the arms are held up in a mute appeal for help and deliverance from all that diminishes life. It has become a symbol to me of the different types of prayer.

This issue of the *Christian Companion* considers many aspects of the life of prayer to which we are called. Each of the 15 contributors explains what prayer means to them, the part it plays in their lives, and how it affects the wider world with which they come into contact. Yvonne Walker discusses the difficulties we have, in a noisy world, to be still enough for long enough to feel and be aware of God's presence, and suggests ways that we can attain a calmer centre for our lives. Ann Lewin and John Pritchard maintain that we really do not have to try too hard: prayer should be a relationship between God and ourselves, and spending time with God and letting

1

ourselves simply 'be' in God's presence maintains that relationship. Andrew Clitherow takes this a step further: if we are willing to embrace powerlessness and poverty in a world obsessed with materialism and possessions, we can discover a new reliance on God and hear what God is trying to say to us in the silence.

Two contributors – Liz Babbs and Lorna Lackenby – use the example of mobile phone technology to illustrate the need to stay in constant touch with God through prayer, and what happens when we feel out of touch, when prayer seems difficult. Jackie Stead and Pam Pointer consider Jesus' life of prayer, in the Lord's Prayer and in the example he gives us of daily bringing everything before God, his life and all it contained constantly linked to the times he spent with his Father.

Robert Dolman discusses the treasures of prayer to be found in the Psalms, in the way they speak to us today of the human condition and our need of God's care and help; and Rod Garner writes of 'praying from the heart', remembering the evocative poetry and grandeur of the prayers of the Church, which reach down the centuries to sustain us in good times and bad.

A number of contributors move us on from the interior life of prayer to prayer for others. Frank Collier discusses the value of our intercessions, and the paradox that praying for others makes it easier to pray for ourselves. Geoffrey Duncan's article is an urgent call to prayer that must result in action, that should make us aware of the great need about us and spur us on to do something about it. Deborah Douglas, too, feels that, while we can legitimately pray that God will preserve us and keep us, we must then offer that care and compassion to others.

Towards the end of the book, John Davies considers the reassurance to be found in an enduring relationship with God, using the service of Compline with its prayers of safekeeping during the night hours. He asserts that, no matter what life throws at us, we have a sure foundation in God's eternal changelessness. Finally, John Lampard asks us to consider which prayers we would like others to use when we die. Far from being morbid, he maintains that there is great comfort to be found in such an exercise, in finding prayers that reflect our ongoing journey into the next stage of life with our Lord.

When we find prayer difficult, it is reassuring to think of others who are praying. Often we can be helped by the prayers of people we do not even know, and we become aware, with Tennyson, that

> More things are wrought by prayer than this world
> dreams of ...
> For so the whole round earth is every way
> Bound by golden chains about the feet of God.

Susan Hibbins
Editor, *The Christian Companion*

Sunbathing

John Pritchard

I've thought of prayer in all sorts of ways. When I was young I saw prayer as a way of getting things I really wanted, and getting them fast. Like the little boy who popped his head round the door and said: 'I'm going to bed now and I'll be saying my prayers. Anybody want anything?' As I got older I thought prayer was a technique you could learn, but those who became proficient at it looked rather pale and wan, and they floated a few inches off the ground, so I was a bit wary of it. Later still I began to see prayer as a relationship of trust and intimacy with an utterly reliable and loving Father.

But recently I've begun to see that one of the simplest and most useful ways of understanding prayer is to see it as being like sunbathing. The essential thing about sunbathing is that you just go and lie in the sun. You don't have to learn a technique. You can't do anything to increase the power of the sun to get a richer tan. You don't have to believe a lot of scientific facts about the sun before you can benefit from it. You just have to go to the right place and lie in it. The sun does the rest.

Prayer is like that. You don't have to have an A level in Spirituality to pray. You can't turn up the power of God's love to feel even warmer. You don't even have to know a lot about

God before you pray. You just have to go to the right place and stay there. Like Woody Allen's famous quip: 'Eighty per cent of life is just turning up.' Just turn up and God will do the rest.

Our biggest problem, then, is turning up. And staying there. We're past masters at finding excuses for not coming to pray. How often I've convinced myself in the early morning that I've just got to get to my desk to finish off that piece of work rather than go and be still in God's presence. I know he's as present at my desk as in my special place of prayer (see Brother Lawrence for details of 'practising the presence of God'). But if you're going to get a tan you have to go and lie in the sun! We spend so much time rushing around inside the house – organizing our lives, tidying up, entertaining others, worrying – that the idea of going out and lying in the sun strikes us as ridiculously self-indulgent. But the result is that our lives are increasingly chaotic.

The first and almost the only thing we have to do, therefore, is to slow down and go outside. The sun gives light throughout the house but it warms you right through when you go out and lie in it. OK, you need a little preparation – a towel and some sun-cream perhaps – but that's all. When we go to pray we may need a candle or a Bible or an icon, maybe some music, but basically we're just going to open ourselves up to the source of Light. God does the rest.

Slowing down is a major problem in our society. We live under the tyranny of speed. Look how the word 'instant' or 'express' is used in marketing. From speed-dating to instant credit, from Pizza Express to Photo Express, from house makeovers to personal makeovers – everything has to be fast. We pack more and more into the same number of hours that our ancestors had, but there is scant evidence of our being happier. There's a deep need for our society to be detoxified from its busyness.

We need to learn the secret that God doesn't rush. He walks at three miles an hour, a humane speed, the speed of love, the speed of the spirit. No one says of a Beethoven symphony that if it was played 25 per cent faster we could squeeze another piece into the concert. It has its own proper speed. The pianist Arthur Schnabel once said: 'The notes I handle no better than many pianists. But the pauses between the notes – ah, that's where art resides.'

The art of praying resides in slowing up sufficiently to be able to bathe in God's warmth and light. Sunbathing.

It seems to me that our society is actually recognizing its need of a slower pace but doesn't know how to find it. There are more self-help courses and books, more therapies and 'natural' remedies, more stress-busting techniques and alternative spiritualities now than ever. But they can look suspiciously like yet more lifestyle choices to add to the clutter of already fragmented lives.

Not surprisingly, Christian wisdom has been there before. St Augustine put it neatly in his famous prayer: 'O God, you have made us for yourself and our souls are restless until they find their rest in you.' We just need to return to the ancient art of sunbathing.

But what do we actually do when we get there and make time for this encounter with the loving nature of the living God? Well – how long is a piece of string? We do whatever we want to do. But some things have been well tried and proved their worth.

a. *We may feel called to use words.* We may simply muse with God and talk with him 'as with a friend', as Moses did (Exodus 33.11). We may find the shape and clarity of a 'daily office' helps, with all its Scripture, psalm and prayer. We may find a bottle of TCP helps, representing Thanksgiving, Confession and Petition. I often return to this simple image when prayer dries up or gets tangled. But words may also hide us from God. Our Sunday worship is usually crazily full of words and the incessant talking often carries over into our private prayer. But it's like applying too much sun-cream when we sunbathe. It simply blocks out the sun.

b. *We may feel called to use our imagination.* We may be drawn to enter into some of the great biblical stories and experience them from the inside – what's called Ignatian meditation. In this way we may see, smell, hear, touch the gospel narrative and so watch the event from the inside rather than reading it from the outside. Or we may bring our special people to Jesus at the well (John 4), and then step back and see what he does. Or we may go on a visit in our imagination to someone who we know is in need, and care for them and offer them to God. Or we may let music carry us into praise, or we might write to God about what's going on in our lives, or we might paint or use modelling clay. The sky's the limit when we're praying with all we've got.

c. *We may feel called to be silent.* Here we reach the simplest and yet most challenging form of sunbathing. Here we may use a favourite biblical phrase which we throw into the pool of silence when we need to, watching the ripples gently make their way outwards, but essentially we're letting God be God in us; we're letting the sun be the sun and give us the tan which grows imperceptibly richer. In Christian terms it's called holiness. But at the same time, being still and silent is challenging because all our 'learned activism' rises up within us and demands that we stop wasting time and get on with life. It's hard to be still. We enter an inner landscape that's unfamiliar and often painful to explore. Living with ourselves isn't easy, and yet this is the restless soul we inflict innocently on others for hours at a time! But it's the experience of so many Christians that this time of stilling and waiting and longing gradually becomes absolutely central to their spiritual health.

The central image of prayer that I offer here is that of sunbathing. And the central problem with that in our restless culture is the difficulty of turning up and staying there, in the sun.

A rabbi looked out over the town square and everywhere he saw people rushing. He called out to one man, 'What are you rushing for?' The man said, 'I'm running to make a living.' The rabbi said, 'What makes you so sure your living is in front of you so that you have to rush to catch up? What if it's behind you? Maybe you should stop and let it catch up with you.'

The sun isn't up ahead of us, over the horizon. It's right overhead. Now.

Thou art our peace, O Lord.
From the thousand wearinesses of our daily life, from the
disappointments, from nervous and senseless haste, we turn
to thee and are at peace. The clamour dies, and we are alive
in the sunshine of thy presence. Even so come, Lord Jesus, to
this soul of mine.

Anonymous

℘　℃　℘

As for prayer, don't burden yourself with making
considerations, neither your mind nor mine is
good at that. Follow your own way of speaking to
our Lord sincerely, lovingly, confidently, and
simply, as your heart dictates.

Jane de Chantal

℘　℃　℘

Pray temperately and simply. Prayer is a heart-to-heart talk
between yourself and God and needs no brilliant ideas, no
flood of words.

Anonymous

So many Christians have lost touch with their own tradition of prayer. We no longer benefit as we should from the wisdom and experienced counsel of the great masters of prayer. All these masters have agreed that in prayer it is not we ourselves who are taking the initiative. We are not talking to God. We are listening to his word among us. We are not looking for him; it is he who has found us. Walter Hilton expressed it very simply in the fourteenth century. He wrote: 'You, yourself, do nothing, you simply allow him to work in your soul!'... The advice of St Theresa was in tune with this. She reminds us that all we can do in prayer is to dispose ourselves; the rest is in the power of the Spirit who leads us. ... These teachers (Walter Hilton and St Theresa) have the same experience of prayer as that which led St Paul to write that 'we do not even know how to pray, but the Spirit prays within us' (Romans 8.26) ... He was not writing to specialists in prayer, but to husbands, wives, butchers and bakers.

John Main OSB

Sunbathing

Come now,
turn aside for a while from your daily employment,
escape for a moment from the tumult of your thoughts.
Put aside your weighty cares,
let your burdensome distractions wait,
free yourself awhile for God
and rest awhile in him.
Enter the inner chamber of your soul,
shut out everything except God
and that which can help you in seeking him,
and when you have shut the door, seek him.

St Anselm

Ꭷ Ꮳ Ꭷ

I do a lot of listening. Prayer, you know, is not meant to be a monologue, but a dialogue. It is a communion, a friendly talk. While the Lord communicates with me mainly through his word, he gives me a great deal of comfort ... assurance of his presence with me, and his pleasure in my service.

Samuel Logan Brendle

There is hardly ever a complete silence in our soul. God is whispering to us well-nigh incessantly. Whenever the sounds of the world die out in the soul, or sink low, then we hear those whisperings of God. He is always whispering to us, only we do not always hear, because of the noise, hurry, and distraction which life causes at it rushes on.

Frederick W. Faber

When we pray, the simpler our prayers are the better; the plainest, humblest language which expresses our meaning is the best.

C.H. Spurgeon

A compass for our lives

Jackie Stead

I am currently absorbed by a prettily packaged book called *House Rules*. It's described as the 'Mrs Beeton of the 21st century' and is full of advice on everything from cleaning your home and organizing your wardrobe, to dress codes for Henley and Royal Ascot, correspondence etiquette and the stress-free way to entertain. It's designed for a generation of women who have never been taught how to cook a Sunday roast or how to iron a shirt, and it's proving incredibly popular. I love books like this, though how much of it I put into practice remains to be seen!

And there's the rub – my home will only become a domestic idyll if I put into action what I've read. It's not enough to know how to achieve streak-free, gleaming windows; if I want to let the sunshine in, I have to actually do something.

I think prayer may have a lot in common with housework. Please don't misunderstand me here. Prayer is first and foremost a wonderful privilege, but it is also a discipline, and one in which many of us fall short. There are many, many books explaining why and how to do it, but if I want to see a real difference in my life, I need to put down those books and start to pray.

I'm tremendously grateful that the disciples asked Jesus to teach them how to pray (Luke 11.1) and that we have Jesus' answer recorded in the gospels. The Lord's Prayer sets the standard for all praying. The late Selwyn Hughes said: 'The more we understand this model, and the more we pray in line with it, the more powerful and productive our prayer life will become.'

A few years ago now, a visiting preacher to our church spoke on the Lord's Prayer and illustrated how we can use it not just to repeat verbatim (though that has value), but as a model to guide our thoughts as we pray. Since then, I have kept coming back to this prayer and the riches contained within it.

We begin 'Our Father ...'. Jesus reminds us that our relationship with God is one of love. He created us and in prayer we can talk and listen to the one who knows us better than we know ourselves. Too often, as Oswald Chambers writes: 'We look upon prayer simply as a means of getting things for ourselves, but the biblical purpose of prayer is that we may get to know God himself.'

These opening words of the Lord's Prayer give us our perspective, but they also teach us to look beyond ourselves. We are told to pray '*Our* Father'. We live in community – in our locality and in the world, and so we are reminded that our prayer is not only for ourselves, but also for others.

I like to pause as I pray 'Hallowed be your name'. This is worship, as we express reverence for all that God is. *The*

Message translates this line as 'Reveal who you are'. There are many names for God in the Bible and each one reveals something of his character and nature. Hagar describes God as El Roi, 'The one who sees me' (Genesis 16.13); to Abraham he is Jehovah Jireh, 'The Lord will provide' (Genesis 22.14) and to David, he is 'My shepherd' (Psalm 23). When we pray 'Hallowed be your name', we might like to ask that God reveals himself to us as our provider, our shepherd, our rock, our healer .... And remembering that we pray '*Our* Father', we can pray along these lines for others whose needs are known to us.

'Your kingdom come' is our response. We are reminded that prayer is not about presenting our shopping list of wants, or asking a blessing on our ideas and plans, it is asking what God would have us do. How might he want to shape our lives? What are his desires for the community in which we worship, for the wider community in which we live and for the world of which we are a part?

Even more challenging is the next part of the prayer: 'Your will be done'. These are words of submission. Here, we bring before God our hopes for ourselves and for others, our frustrations and difficulties, our ambitions and passions. We are led to pray as Jesus prayed in the Garden of Gethsemane: 'Not my will, but yours be done' (Luke 22.42).

'Give us this day our daily bread' reminds us of our dependence on God for all our needs. Everything we have comes from him and we are encouraged to ask him for what we need each day. This, too, comes as a challenge. I like to plan ahead and I'm a worrier. I know I risk missing the blessings of today because I am already worrying about what I need for next week!

On my fridge, I have a magnet which says: 'Today is the tomorrow you worried about yesterday and all is well.' As I pray, 'Give us *this day* ...' I am drawn back to the immediate. I can see how God has provided for me today and I am encouraged to trust him for the future. But there is still more here. We pray '*Give us* this day', so we might also think of other people, less fortunate, praying for their daily bread and consider if we might play a part in God's provision for them.

'Forgive us our sins' speaks of our spiritual dependency on God and our need of his mercy. I find the General Confession used by the Anglican Church is most helpful here. Our sins are both against God and against each other 'in thought and word and deed, in the evil we have done and in the good we have not done, through ignorance, through weakness and through our own deliberate fault'.

It is a sobering prayer and the more so because we ask God to forgive us as we forgive others. Jesus teaches us that the grace we have received from God we must pass on to others – remember the story of the unmerciful servant (Matthew 18.21-35)? So, we must forgive others and be forgiving in our dealings with other people.

Finally, we pray 'Lead us not into temptation, but deliver us from the evil one'. Temptation does not come from God, as the Bible makes clear: 'God cannot be tempted by evil and he himself tempts no one. But one is tempted by one's own desire, being lured and enticed by it' (James 1.13-14). Again, I think *The Message* translation is helpful. It says simply: 'Keep us safe from ourselves and the devil.' We are asking for God's protection over us, that he will constantly draw us to himself, and enable us to stand against anything that would seek to draw us away from his truth.

And so, as we follow the words of the Lord's Prayer, it acts as a compass for our lives. It shows us where we are in our relationship with God – whether we are seeking his will, whether we are depending on him – and where we are with others. Are we passing on the grace we have received and supporting each other in prayer?

We might not always be able to follow the prayer in such detail, but perhaps, at least once a year, rather like a good spring clean in our homes, we can use the words of Jesus to check our lives and ensure that his light can shine clearly through us.

Prayer

Lord,
in your mercy
forgive what we have been,
amend what we are,
and direct what we shall be
for Jesus Christ's sake.
Amen.

New Every Morning

ঙ ও ঙ

We are summoned to a new level of identification. We are
summoned to be disciples, and so to a discipline. A disciple is
a learner and his discipline is the training whereby he learns.
To learn the way of the cross is the hardest thing of all, and
the training by which we are to advance in this learning is
provided for us by the discipline of prayer and worship. Those
who disparage prayer and worship and imagine that without
these one can achieve some kind of instant Christianity do not
know what they are talking about. They understand neither
the weakness of our humanity nor the depth of the richness of
the spiritual maturity into which Christ is calling us.

John Macquarrie

A compass for our lives

In the school of prayer we must be on our guard lest the Lord's Prayer may become so familiar that we lose the beauty and real meaning which it conveys. It supplied a real need which the disciple expressed in his request: 'Lord, teach us to pray.' The Lord's Prayer teaches [us] the right approach to prayer, and opens up a channel of communication with God.

Frederick Wilcox

To be with God wondering, that is adoration. To be with God gratefully, that is thanksgiving. To be with God ashamed, that is contrition. To be with God with others on our heart, that is intercession. The secret is the quest of God's presence: 'Thy face, Lord, will I seek.'

Michael Ramsay

One single grateful thought raised to heaven is the most perfect prayer.

G.E. Lessing

The final end of prayer is not that our
will should be done by God, but that
his will should be done by us.

Alfred Plummer

৪১   ৫১   ৪১

[The Lord's Prayer] is not only a pattern prayer for our
worship, but its themes touch the very heart of our faith and
commitment. The parenthood and holiness of God, the
meaning of the kingdom of God, and the content of God's will
are part of the essential framework of what we believe. The
goodness of God, forgiveness, temptation, suffering and sin
are the very stuff of our Christian experience.

Frank Collier

৪১   ৫১   ৪১

None can believe how powerful prayer is,
and what it is able to effect, but those who
have learned it by experience.

Martin Luther

Given by Jesus [the Lord's Prayer] must be *the* focus of Christian spirituality. Saying it can be cheap; praying it can never be any other than costly. It has few words; it is dense with allusions to faith. In praying through it, we trustingly reach out to the Father whose love and grace, justice and compassion are wrapped up in the phrase 'God is and for us'. In praying as Jesus taught his disciples, we ask little of God, save that we genuinely become God's people.

Peter Doble

Our thanks to God should always precede our requests.

Anonymous

The Lord's Prayer ends with the word amen. This word means 'so be it'. It is a word we use at the end of every prayer. It means we agree, we give our assent. In other words, if we say a prayer we should not only mean it, we should be prepared to live it. We are making a commitment to God and to ourselves. It is for this reason that we should be careful of what we ask for in prayer. God *will* answer!

Stephen Cottrell

Praying by heart

Rod Garner

Olive is one of my regular home communicants. I first met her several years ago as she nursed her sick husband with care and devotion. She is in her eighties now, tires easily and forgets most things fairly quickly. Holy Communion means a great deal to her and we sit quietly in her room as she prepares to receive the bread of heaven. We dispense with books and service leaflets and to put her at ease I always assure her that she will be able to remember the prayers that we shall say together. The small miracle is that she always does. The opening prayer to the God who knows our deepest desires and secrets, the confession, the Our Father and the closing prayer of thanksgiving – all of these and more she is able to recite by heart. She takes comfort from this ability to bring to mind hallowed texts when so much of her past has slipped away from her, and she is visibly moved by their beauty. A single sentence brings her pleasure – 'Come unto me all ye that labour and are heavy laden and I will give you rest' – and for a few minutes she has the sense of being caught up in the great ocean of prayer that represents centuries of Christian tradition. Words, repeated over and over again, retain their ancient power and speak to her of a Love that can be trusted as she approaches journey's end.

Olive, we might say, is fortunate. Her spiritual roots can be traced to a very different era when the young were expected to learn things by heart in the classroom or Sunday school and there was less indifference or ignorance concerning basic Christian truths. Unlike today, children had no difficulty in reciting the Lord's Prayer. I followed the same path a generation later and remain profoundly grateful that similar expectations were laid upon me. More to the point, I grew to love religious words. Singing from the age of eight in a church choir opened the treasure chest of psalms and anthems and I grew familiar with the haunting Collects that related the unfolding drama of the Christian year. I was lured by their language, completely unaware that it represented the 'Church's banquet' – the rich and unceasing flow of prayer that would in time, for me, take on profoundly personal associations. When I heard the words 'Almighty God, give us grace to cast away the works of darkness and put on the armour of light' I knew that Advent had come once more with its evocation of hope and last things. The austerities of Lent were announced by the sobering words of Ash Wednesday beseeching the God of great forbearance to 'create and make in us new and contrite hearts'. As a small boy prone to the usual distractions, daydreams and mischief of the choir stalls I was still enthralled by the imagery of the psalms and how a single phrase was able to fire my imagination and become part of the permanent furniture of my mind. I wanted to know more about Jerusalem 'built as a city'; about the God 'who was our hope and strength, a very present help in trouble'; about the heroic sailors who 'went down to the sea in ships and had their business in great waters'. I rarely tired of singing or reciting these words and they have become my gracious travelling companions, providing me with a vocabulary of prayer that continues to inspire and sustain.

I realize of course that praying by heart or committing to memory the best that has been handed on to us is neither fashionable nor easy in a culture that appears ambivalent concerning the wisdom of the past, views most things as disposable and replaceable and is not at ease with the notion that certain forms of language are better than others precisely because the words remain the same. The Church is not immune from such pressures: for a generation now we have been exposed to freshly minted books of prayers, alternative intercessions, contemporary patterns of worship and an explosion of hymn-writing. New words are being employed to shape our praying and some of them are good. At our Family Service this Sunday I shall ask the children to pay particular attention to verse three of Graham Kendrick's justly famous hymn, 'The Servant King', as it invites us to gaze on 'the scars that speak of sacrifice' and 'the hands that flung stars into space, to cruel nails surrendered'. The imagery moves the heart and the imagination and deserves to be remembered. By contrast however, and this constitutes a serious loss, many of the new words we are being offered are trite and ephemeral, unsuited to their task and unworthy of a Creator deserving of our 'choicest psalmody'. They will not grow with us as we grow older and we shall never care for them or love them more deeply. Until a more durable religious sensibility is rekindled in our common worship, there is every incentive to cherish and learn the prayers that constitute our heritage and point us to the heart of things.

They do more than this, however. Any sustained attempt on our part to live a spiritual life will include the occasions when we find it hard to pray, when our own words fail us and the flesh and the spirit alike are weak. Few of us get to heaven on feather beds and none of us can expect to bypass boredom, depression, the slow or sudden decline of the senses, sickness, grief and, ultimately, the sure knowledge of our death. Praying by heart enables us to withstand the winter's landscape. In a recent interview, Kenneth Stevenson, Bishop of Portsmouth, described his protracted stay in hospital as a cancer patient. He spoke movingly of the days when he could barely see because of the chemotherapy, yet he still persisted with the regular discipline of saying morning and evening prayer and it helped to get him through.

In a lighter vein there are the moments of celebration and wonder when, as the novelist Virginia Woolf writes, we are moved to 'repay life its favours' but we need a better vocabulary than most of us can manage. I am smiling as I write these words: I can see myself standing outside a college some 20 years ago having just completed the last exam in my Philosophy Finals. The whole business of sitting seven different papers in a relatively short space of time and keeping my parish work intact at the same time had rather got to me. After putting my pen down the relief was immense: my life was almost mine again and I had to do something. Taking in the late afternoon air I could do no other than look up and say aloud 'Praise be to the God and Father of our Lord Jesus Christ, who in his great mercy gave us new birth into a living hope by the resurrection of Jesus Christ from the dead!' (1 Peter 1.3). At that precise moment, no other words could have conveyed my feelings so powerfully and accurately and I didn't care if anyone heard! I was free and Scripture gave voice to my liberation!

What I have tried to convey here is that praying by heart is necessary and worthwhile. It is an open secret within the life of the Church and a source of its renewal in confusing times. It is about finding the old way forward – the joyful discipline that does not disappoint us and the discovery of a wisdom that lightens the longest days.

We give thanks to thee, O Lord,
who hast preserved us through the day;
and to thee we pay our vows for protection
     through the coming night;
bring us in safety to the morning hours,
we beseech thee, that so thou mayest at all times
     receive our praise.
Through Christ our Lord, Amen.

Gelasian Sacramentary

Psalm 121 was the one least likely to cause my attention to wander [in church], because the poetry was so good. Those images of the protectiveness of God were arrestingly evocative: the Lord who made heaven and earth never stumbling on his watch, staying close as a shadow, preventing even a foot from sliding, keeping the soul safe.

Sally Magnusson

Certain thoughts are prayers. There are moments when, whatever be the attitude of the body, the soul is on its knees.

Victor Hugo

Prayer

Green lichen clinging to cut granite stones,
Grey sunlight streaming through glass,
Dust dancing on polished oak pews,
Lingering dreams of the past.
Hush as you enter. Walk softly my dear,
Kneel at the altar and pray,
For this is a house where many have come,
And where Christ has chosen to stay.

Pat Robson

        ℬ   ☙   ℬ

'Well, Master Marner, it's niver too late to turn over a new
leaf, and if you've niver had no church, there's no telling the
good it'll do you. For I feel so set up and comfortable as niver
was, when I've been and heard the prayers, and the singing
to the praise and glory o' God, as Mr Macey gives out – and
Mr Crackenthorp saying good words, and more partic'lar on
Sacrament day; and if a bit o' trouble comes, I feel as I can
put up wi' it, for I've looked for help i' the right quarter.'

George Eliot

I am glad that I was taken to church regularly, initiated into the Christian faith, and helped to participate in the profound poetry of the Christian year. Though inattentive I came insensibly to know the liturgy word for word, and to live in the double rhythm of the earthly seasons and of man's noblest imaginings. ... The Collect for Advent Sunday was the first Collect for the day I was set to learn by heart. I determined to be word perfect. We said the Collect to my mother on Sunday mornings. It was not easy to learn and nothing was explained – excessive explanation is the wicked fairy in modern education. For me there was no tarnishing process; the rhythmic prose swung unchipped into my mind:

> Almighty God, give us grace that we may cast away the works of darkness, and put upon us the armour of light, now in the time of this mortal life, in which Thy Son Jesus Christ came to visit us in great humility; that in the last day, when He shall come again in his glorious majesty to judge both the quick and the dead, we may rise to the life immortal. Through him who livest and reignest with Thee and the Holy Ghost, now and for ever. Amen.

I did not know how grand it was, I was only exultant that I was learning it. I shouted it to the thorns and to the wind; and my mother, when I repeated it on Sunday, said it was good.

Anne Treneer

Prayer

Shadows and coolness, Lord, art thou to me;
Cloud of my soul, lead on, I follow thee.
What though the hot winds blow,
Fierce heat beat up below,
Fountains of water flow –
Praise, praise to thee.

Clearness and glory, Lord, art thou to me;
Light of my soul, lead on, I follow thee.
All through the moonless night,
Making its darkness bright,
Thou art my heavenly light –
Praise, praise to thee.

Shadows and shine art thou, dear Lord, to me;
Pillar of cloud and fire, I follow thee.
What though the way be long,
In thee my heart is strong,
Thou art my joy, my song –
Praise, praise to thee.

Amy Carmichael

Follow the leader

Pam Pointer

Each week my local newspaper carries a column in which someone in the community is asked a range of 20 trivial and serious questions. 'Which actor would you like to portray you in a film?' 'Do you have your own website?' 'What are the last three places you went to for a holiday?' ... and, 'Do you pray?'

Well, do *you* pray? Yes, no, sometimes, never, only in a crisis, all the time ...

Christianity is a relationship – between God and human beings. Prayer is all about communication, the most vital aspect of any relationship. Jesus was constantly in touch with his Father through prayer. What an example!

So let's 'follow the leader' and enjoy the exciting and challenging voyage of discovery about prayer. Skim through a gospel at one sitting and take note of every time prayer is mentioned. Feel the increased momentum of events unfolding during the three years of Jesus' ministry. It's like a good movie where the tension increases and the pace quickens as you watch the action. And prayer, as Jesus demonstrates, is paramount.

Who prays, to whom, and for whom?

Jesus prayed. Synagogue and Temple priests prayed, the disciples prayed, crowds prayed, individuals prayed. They prayed to God. They prayed for friends and for enemies, for unnamed groups, for individuals.

Where?

In a place of worship
Different places for different purposes. Jesus prayed in the synagogue and in the Temple. Whether we are in a crowd or, as Jesus also suggested, with two or three people, we are encouraged and inspired to pray and worship together.

Behind a closed door
For personal and private prayer it is appropriate to be alone and quiet, to shut the door on distractions and be with God alone. It's an attractive prospect, surely, to have time and a space in which to have uncluttered communication with God. Jesus recognized and wants us to recognize the importance of such one-to-one encounters.

In lonely places
Jesus often chose 'lonely places' to pray on his own. What are your chosen lonely places? Do you prefer, as it seems Jesus did, the outdoor places, rather than indoors? A nearby hill is my favourite place. The vastness of the sky reminds me of God as Creator, whether at sunrise, sunset, in the wind and rain or when the first stars appear – the uncluttered beauty of God's creation. A line of electric pylons or the sound of traffic may

be present but it is God who predominates in that open-air space. Jesus loved the hills, finding the outward manifestation of the Creator's work a focal point to concentrate on God.

In a garden
Jesus prayed in the Garden of Gethsemane. On the last occasion it wasn't a pretty place of solace, but a place of agony and struggle. It is our solace to know that Jesus knows what ultimate suffering is and that he can empathize with us when we struggle and suffer.

On the cross
Jesus prayed when he was dying on the cross – but, extraordinarily, for others rather than for himself. 'Father, forgive them,' he prayed, 'for they don't know what they're doing.' We hear of relatives praying, in their grief, for the perpetrators of murder or violence. In his own agony of body, Jesus prayed for other people. And at the last, as he died, he committed his spirit into the safe hands of his Father.

When?

Early
Jesus' schedule was hectic. He got up at daybreak, left the demands of the town of Capernaum, and went off to a lonely place to pray (Luke 4.42). Even so, the people jumped out of bed to go looking for him. What demands are made on your day? Young children to feed, clothe and get to school? An early start to get to work? Elderly parents to care for? After giving out, batteries need to be recharged. Exercise,

paradoxically, reinvigorates a tired body, and the exercise of communication with God reinvigorates tired minds and souls. The greater the demands on us, the greater our need to have time alone with God.

Late

Jesus sometimes spent an entire night in prayer! One occasion was just before he chose his 12 disciples. With today's emphasis on celebrity, power and status, we might think he chose an unlikely bunch. He chose them after prayer. God can do extraordinary things with 'ordinary' people. When we have an important matter to deal with in the church, at home or at work, would we consider staying up all night to pray about it?

Jesus prayed all night when he was in Jerusalem. This was a tense episode in the movie when the action was getting faster, more sinister, more dangerous. He'd expended energy in teaching in the Temple, his enemies were plotting against him, and the situation was rolling towards crisis point. Jesus knew it and spent time with his Father.

Always

At that uneasy time Jesus told his disciples to persist in prayer. 'Be alert at all times, praying that you may have the strength to escape all these things that will take place, and to stand before the Son of Man' (Luke 21.36).

How?

Jesus prayed simply, and urged his disciples to do the same. There's no need to be long-winded or use complicated language. Jesus spoke in language that people understood. He spoke naturally and with humility. How sensible of the disciples to ask for Jesus' help in prayer. His model, the Lord's Prayer, was simplicity itself.

What?

Praise!
There's a lovely example of Jesus praying joyfully. He'd welcomed back the 72 people who'd been out sharing the good news. He saw their joy, heard their excited tales of what had happened and 'was filled with joy by the Holy Spirit'. He praised God for the men and women who were helping him. Does Jesus praise God with joy for *your* part in sharing his good news?

Thank you!
Jesus thanked God for his provision of daily needs. Do you give thanks, as Jesus did, for the food that you have at each meal? Do you thank him when you recover from a cold, from an accident, or when there's some good news in the family?

Please!
Jesus asked for release from suffering when in the Garden of Gethsemane. How often do we ask for our suffering to be taken from us? Sometimes the suffering is taken away; often it isn't. It wasn't removed for Jesus. He would suffer more than

any other human being has ever done or will ever do. We may not find release from suffering but, like Jesus, we may know God's strength *in* suffering. An angel came to Jesus to give him strength. We too may pray for God's presence and strength in our suffering and in the suffering of our loved ones. Just as a child asks his daddy for things, so God wants us to ask him for advice, for help, for our needs, for other people ....

Sorry!
We confess to God when we stumble in our daily walk with him and, because of Jesus, we receive forgiveness.

Enjoy the effects of prayer:

God's presence
God's provision
God's power
God's purpose
God's peace.

Follow the leader

O Christ, our dearest Saviour,
kindle our lamps
that they may evermore shine in your temple
and receive unquenchable light from you
that will lighten our darkness
and lessen the darkness of the world.

Attributed to Saint Columba

ဢ ဢ ဢ

It is Jesus who moves us to pray. He knocks. Thereby he makes known his desire to come in to us. Our prayers are always a result of Jesus' knocking at our hearts' doors.

O. Hallesby

ဢ ဢ ဢ

Get into the habit of dealing with God about everything. Unless in the first waking moment of the day you learn to fling the door wide back and let God in, you will work on a wrong level all day; but swing the door wide open and pray to God in secret, and every public thing will be stamped with the presence of God.

Oswald Chambers

Abruptly, Jesus turned and stepped through a cleft in the valley wall and was gone. No one tried to follow him – not even Simon ... Andrew no longer worried about Jesus. Perhaps because his own shy spirit suffered in the blunt, boisterous self-confident public, he seemed to understand his master's withdrawals. The most significant decisions must be made in private. The hardest knots must be loosed in solitary prayer. Andrew descended the mountain thinking *Jesus is praying. He has found a lonely cove, and he is praying.*

Walter Wangerin

> If our hearts are thus lifted up to him, centred upon him, filled with his fullness and strength, our lives must cheer and help others too, simply because he is there.

Kathleen Alice Orr

I believe that as, from time to time, our Lord found it necessary to go apart to a quiet place and pray from his heart, he not only prayed that he might not lose the sense of his Father's presence, but he prayed too – and I hope I am not being blasphemous in the suggestion – he prayed too that his Father would understand that he, Jesus, was doing his best.

Donald Soper

Every prayer-filled day sees a meeting with the God who comes; every night which we faithfully put at his disposal is full of his presence. And his waiting and his presence are not only the result of our waiting or a prize for our efforts: they are his decision, based on his love freely poured out.

Carlo Carretto

ಬಿ   ಲ   ಬಿ

This is the miracle I seek,
O Living Christ,
Your strength and purpose in my hands,
Your kindness in my voice,
Within my heart your certainty of God,
Your love for all mankind.

George MacLeod

ಬಿ   ಲ   ಬಿ

If we want to grow in faith and in the school of prayer we have but one example and inspiration. If Jesus, in all his goodness, sought to do the will of his Father as the foundation of his communion with him, so ought we. Regardless of the outcome.

James Jones

Prayer

Lord Jesus Christ,
alive and at large in the world,
help me to follow and find you there today
in the places where I work,
meet people, spend money
and make plans.
Take me as a disciple of your kingdom
and see through your eyes
and hear the questions you are asking,
to welcome all with your trust and truth,
and to change the things that contradict God's love
by the power of your cross
and the freedom of your Spirit.

Anonymous

Another lesson I learned was that the intensity of prayer is not measured by time, but by the reality and depth of one's awareness of unity with God. I learned to look on prayer not as a means of influencing the Creator in my favour, but as an awareness of the presence of God – everywhere.

Margaret Bondfield

Listening to God in silence

Yvonne Walker

We tend to look on prayer as talking to God, saying our prayers. However, prayer involves listening as well as speaking, but so often *we* do all the talking and God doesn't get a word in edgeways. Someone once commented that it is not so much the gift of tongues as the gift of ears that we need. Prayer is about listening – listening to myself and listening to God, a type of attentiveness which brings me into relationship with God. In silent prayer we are invited by a beckoning God to let God be God and let ourselves be who we are too.

Silence is nothing new in the Hebrew scriptures. 'Be still, and know that I am God!' is probably the best-known passage about silent prayer (Psalm 46.10). 'Be still before the Lord, and wait patiently for him' (Psalm 37.7) is another favourite quotation. I'm sure you can find many more.

Silent prayer is about **being not doing**. It is not primarily something I *do*, but something God is doing in me. Simply being with God in silence like this can be a very natural way of praying. It may be the only way we can pray when we are tired or ill. Some children instinctively pray in this way. So did the old man who explained why he spent a lot of time sitting in church for hours on end: 'I look at him and he looks at me.'

The person who prays silently ceases activity *not* in order to be idle and lazy, but to enter into the activity of God. Silence is not vacant or negative; it is not just about the absence of noise. The type of silence found in reflective prayer is positive and involves being receptive in stillness and quiet. The silence and solitude is nourishing for the soul – it is in the depths of this silence that we draw refreshment, strength and encouragement to give ourselves to others. By going to the quiet places, the oasis of our busy lives, we are renewed, gain strength and are sustained.

Even the busiest and most pressured person can find silence in their lives if they value the chance to pause and desire to spend time with God. With a little creativity and ingenuity time *can* be set aside even in the busiest lifestyles. This may not necessarily mean physical aloneness but rather finding interior space to reflect on where God is in our busy lives. It may be standing in a bus queue, sitting on a train or waiting in a traffic jam. The more frenetic our activity the fewer are the opportunities for silence and solitude. Our spirit cries out for space just to be, and the risk is that we ignore that desire to listen to God in the stillness.

In today's busy and noisy world we are bombarded with an enormous amount of sound stimulation. We have become used to constant noise and background Muzak wherever we are. The Walkman has been replaced by the iPod so that thousands of our favourite tunes are available through earphones just at the touch of a button. The external pressures on our ability to listen in an increasingly noisy world make silent prayer extremely difficult. Yet it is something we long for: to have a few moments' peace and quiet in order to become aware of God's presence and draw near in relationship to the God who loves us.

Silence is about **letting go**. When I talk to God in prayer I set the agenda, I choose what I am going to say, I am very much in control. In silent prayer all this falls away. I need to let go my fears and apprehensions, my impatience, my busyness, my desire to always be on the go. In the silence my ego and any delusions I might have of self-importance are cut down to size by handing over to God the need to prove myself. Our response to the stress of modern life should not be putting in more and more effort but simply letting go and letting God. We can let go the need to live our lives in a way that would merit a special badge or a gold star, we can stop striving after perfection. Silent prayer invites me to ask questions about letting go: 'What do I hang on to? What can I let go? Where is my security? What is getting in the way between me and God? What is all that baggage of worries and concerns that I carry around with me? Can I really trust God enough to let it all go in the silence?'

Silence is also about **distractions.** As soon as we begin to focus on God our mind fills with all sorts of thoughts. Did I lock the front door when I left home? What shall we have for dinner? I must remember to get my new season ticket. Our mind is quite normally full of thoughts and distractions going on the whole time. So how do we deal with these distractions when we want to focus on silent prayer?

Different people suggest different ways for dealing with distractions. Some suggest that if you just ignore them, they will eventually go away. Others say you can keep a notebook beside you so that you can make a note of them and then let them go. There are also some imaginative techniques when you can imagine you post the thoughts through a letter-box. Or you stand on a bridge above a river and drop the thoughts into the water beneath. Or you can draw some little boxes and label them 'my anxiety', 'my jobs-to-do list', 'my desire to control', then let them go. It's important to find a method which suits you.

There may be some concerns about friends or family which we are reluctant to drop – these we can gently hand over to God's safe keeping during our time of prayer to be picked up afterwards. So when your mind wanders, as it will, just bring it back gently to the focus of your prayer. It can also be helpful to return to focus on your breathing.

Finally, silence is about **connectedness**. God does not exist in isolation and we are not solitary individuals, cut off from each other. Contemplative prayer is sometimes accused of being too individualistic, navel gazing, a private self-indulgence, unconcerned with the needs of others. I would suggest instead that in silent prayer we experience a gradual process of self-offering. We offer ourselves in the stillness to God before we get involved in works of concern for others. Silent prayer is a channel for God's unseen operation in the world and, far from avoiding engagement, it empowers and strengthens our contemplative living and commitment to serve, following the example of Christ.

Strong silence
warm silence
loud silence
loving silence

nurture me
enfold me

fill me, still me
write your will in me

align me

with the sacred unity.

Pat Marsh

When you pray, rather let your heart be without words than your words without heart.

John Bunyan

The more we receive in silent prayer, the more we can give in our active life. We need silence to be able to touch souls. The essential thing is not what we say, but what God says to us and through us. All our words will be useless unless they come from within – words which do not give the light of life increase the darkness.

Mother Teresa

When your heart is wandering and distracted, bring it back quietly to its point, restore it tenderly to its Master's side; and if you did nothing else the whole of your hour but bring back your heart patiently and put it near our Lord again, and every time you put it back it turned away again, your hour would be well-employed.

St Francis de Sales

ะ&ว&ะ&ะ

For most of us prayer is often quite hard and sometimes impossible. We can't help wondering whether God is really interested in the everyday doings of our little lives. We can't help wondering whether he's there at all, or whether we're simply wasting our time. Our thoughts disappear into an open sky, or bounce back at us from the ceiling.

All of us who pray have this experience. There are times – perhaps even long periods of time – when we seem to be waiting for God. All we can say of him is that he doesn't seem to be around. But as we continue to be available to him, we become aware that he is in fact all around us – and within us. He is everywhere and very close.

Andrew Knowles

Sometimes when I pray, I utter the words,
But I do not feel or think them.
Sometimes when I pray, I utter the words,
Thinking about what I say, but not feeling.
Sometimes when I pray, I utter the words,
And I both think and feel what I say.

An act of will cannot make me feel,
Nor stop my mind from wandering.
An act of will can only make me utter.
So I shall utter the words,
And let the Spirit do the rest,
Guiding my mind and heart as he wills.

Robert Van de Weyer

Does God have a set way of prayer, that he expects each of us to follow? I doubt it. I believe some people – lots of people – pray through the witness of their lives, through the work they do, the friendships they have, the love they offer people and receive from people. Since when are words the only acceptable form of prayer?

Dorothy Day

Prayer

There is a contemplative in all of us,
almost strangled but still alive,
who craves quiet enjoyment of the Now
and longs to touch the seamless
garment of silence
which makes us whole.

                                    Alan P. Torey

God is our true Friend, who always gives us the counsel and
comfort we need. Our danger lies in resisting him; so it is
essential that we acquire the habit of hearkening to his voice,
or keeping silence within, and listening so as to lose nothing
of what he says to us. We know well enough how to keep
outward silence, and to hush our spoken words, but we know
little of interior silence. It consists in hushing our idle,
restless, wandering imagination, in quieting the promptings of
our worldly minds, and in suppressing the crowd of
unprofitable thoughts which excite and disturb the soul.

                                    François Fénelon

*Deepest communion with God is
beyond words, on the other side
of silence.*

                    Madeleine L'Engle

Prayer in action

Geoffrey Duncan

I cannot live as if justice is of no importance.

Lord of my motivation
Encourage me to keep going
Enable me to be ever more
Determined to work for what
I believe
Might be ...
Justice.

I cannot live as if justice is of no importance.

When I see people on a television screen:
The women
     The men
          The children
Injured
     Distraught
          Bereaved
All certainly traumatized ...

They are flesh and blood ...
With human feelings ...

Suffering ...
according to the ways
and understanding in which they live their lives.

I cannot live as if justice is of no importance.

Thank you for the investigative journalists
the television reporters
the women and men who put their lives on the line ...
so that we might see and have some knowledge
... and try to understand ...
Thank you to the One who seeks to protect them.

I cannot live as if justice is of no importance.

The contemporary Church, set in fast-changing global situations, needs to appeal to the consciences of all people to demonstrate the increasing need for prayer in action. James got it right when he announced that faith without action is dead (James 2.17).

An increasing number of women, men and children are terrified for their lives, especially when they are refused permission to stay in this country, having fled repressive regimes, or circumstances in which, if they return, they will be tortured and murdered by forces in their own country.

Prayer in action is seen when a minister and her husband leaflet an airport against a young person being deported on the next flight to Afghanistan. It is seen when the pilot of the plane refuses to fly the young person back to Afghanistan and as a result his case is reopened. After months of mental agony the young man was given leave to stay in Britain. If various people had not put their necks on the block and their careers on the line by prayer in action then the young Afghani in all likelihood would be dead.

There are many people working today for a new heaven on a new earth. This can become a reality in the lives of millions of people who are marginalized because of their social background, various disabilities, and other forms of discrimination. They are crying out for justice, whether it is in the form of clean water; food for the starving millions; or care for the women, men and the orphaned children living with the reality of HIV/AIDS in Africa, India and western nations. And there are others who cry out for justice: people who, because of their sexuality, are bullied and treated in abhorrent ways by homophobic groups; people who live in the wrong postcode area and cannot receive adequate medical treatment. The list continues ... please add your own relevant concerns. There are people of all faiths who are active vocally and in taking practical action they breathe new life for suffering people. The richness of new living is waiting to be explored. Women ... men ... children whose lives need support from Christians alongside all faith communities – with no strings attached – are crying out for justice.

Let's go with James.

They came to tea

They came to tea.
We shared food and conversation together
and caught a glimpse of the
Love of God.

They shared stories of their lives.
We listened to each other
and learned anew of the
Compassion of Christ.

They presented a challenge.
We talked about ways of living together
and came near the reconciling
Spirit of Justice, Joy and Peace.

Let us celebrate and share
love, compassion and justice.

Mudamma is nineteen. She has polio and lives in a very
remote community in northern Karnataka, south India.
Mudamma lives in a small house, with a banana-leaf roof,
which is shared with a dog, a chicken and a cow. It is in a very
poor state of repair caused by weather conditions and age.

Festival times are good for business because she can at least
make saris to sell to the other women in the village. Most of
the year she and her husband have to rely on growing crops.
The land is parched in rural northern Karnataka. Mudamma

and her husband can't grow enough crops to feed the whole family, including her mother, and have enough left over to sell at the local market. Her husband has to go away to Pune or Mumbai to try and earn a living as a migrant worker. Most times he returns with nothing – there is no work to be had. They have a young daughter to care for – what is the future for her?

Here too is Ramesh who peddles away all day just to get a trickle of polluted water from a nearby well to irrigate his small area of land. He tries to grow crops for food for his family and for sale in the local community. Water is in such short supply – there is never enough for the whole of his tiny plot.

Year on year, his crops fail.

Ramesh and his family live five hundred kilometres from where rich tourists swim in their hotel pools.

Unacceptable ... Obscene

A two-year-old girl was sleeping on the pavement
    of a Tanzanian city.

**Forgive us as we watch
    and continue our lives in bewilderment.**

This two-year-old girl had her toes eaten away by rats as she slept.

Forgive us as we watch
    and feel revulsion because our sensitivities are
    damaged.

This precious two-year-old girl is unable to walk.

Forgive us as we watch
    and get on with what we are doing.

Living Lord ... make us more aware of this ... please give our senses a jolt ... let us know that it is unacceptable for a two-year-old child to be subjected to this obscenity so we:

stand up
make our feet walk
speak out
make our voices heard
listen to the needs of the world
make our hearing far more aware
see the desperate needs of the world
make our seeing more relevant

and for – no, not God's sake, nor for the sake of our Lord Jesus Christ, but for the sake of humankind spurred on by a Loving God ... Compassionate Christ ... Creative Spirit.

Dialling G for God

Liz Babbs

My 'quiet' is so regularly intruded upon by the noise of mobile phones that I have become increasingly irritated by them and the seemingly inane conversations that seem to take place. Okay, yes I admit it, I have one too! However, last year, whilst travelling on a train back from Scotland, my irritation turned to inspiration as I had what Oprah Winfrey describes as 'a light bulb moment'.

When I learned how to meditate some 16 years ago, Joyce Huggett, my vicar's wife, spoke of 'tuning in' to God like a radio, adjusting the dial until you could hear God speak. It was like trying to find his frequency. However, with the digital revolution radios rarely have dials, and a station is automatically found as it scans through the frequencies. If only hearing from God were so easy!

Still, I've found that another, more recent technological device, the mobile phone, has really helped me to have a much fuller understanding of the importance of prayer and meditation in my life and to communicate this to others. Like mobile communication, our relationship with God is dynamic; it's every day, every hour, every minute and so can be every bit as 'cool' and exciting. Wouldn't it be great if people spent as much time with God as they do making calls or sending text messages!

My first mobile phone, affectionately described as 'a brick', was not as 'high tech' as my new one, but that old phone gave me a lot of on-screen information and served as a reminder of six ways in which mobile communication can teach us to communicate more effectively with God.

Switching on ...

First, before you can use a mobile phone, you have to switch it on. In the same way we have to take time to switch on to God, to show our willingness to spend time with him. Just expressing to him your openness is a start, as in this simple prayer:

> *Lord, help me to focus on you,*
> *as we spend time together today.*
> *Renew my mind and help me to let go*
> *of all the clutter that gets in the way.*

Registering ...

Next, my mobile phone has to take a few seconds to register its connection to the phone system, which is a reminder to me to acknowledge my own connectedness to God. You need to admit your dependence on that connection.

Lord, you are my Father and Saviour,
Creator and Lord
Apart from you
I can do
nothing.

Searching ...

Then my mobile tells me that it is searching for the particular person I am trying to call. It is trying to find his or her signal. This is like tuning in to God's presence, taking time just to quiet and hear that 'still small voice' of God. But if I hear nothing, I have not failed, because even wasting time with the one we love is valuable. In fact, it's at the heart of prayer. As lovers grow in intimacy and love, words become unnecessary, and, to quote one retreatant, 'Silence says all'. We don't spend time with God for what we can get from Him. Wasting time with God is always an investment. One day we will have nothing but time to spend with God – so our quiet times and Sabbath rests are preparation for heaven.

Signal strength low ...

Tiredness, stress, anxiety, illness, relationship difficulties, interruptions, children screaming in another room etc., will all interfere with our ability to focus on God. Somehow, we have to learn how to ignore the internal and external noises, or incorporate them in such a way that they no longer become a distraction.

Battery low ...

What a wonderful reminder *battery low* is. My mobile phone will only function for twenty-four hours before it displays this warning. At this point I have to recharge its batteries by plugging it into an electricity source.

In the same way we have to keep coming back to base, returning to our Source, which is God. This is exactly what Jesus did when he took time out to be with his Father: *'After leaving them, he [Jesus] went up on a mountain to pray'* (Mark 6.36).

The pattern of ministering and withdrawal, giving out and then receiving, is Biblical. It was modelled by Jesus and Jesus encouraged his disciples to adopt this same pattern. *'Then, because so many people were coming and going that they did not even have chance to eat, he said to them "Come with Me by yourselves to a quiet place and get some rest" ' (Mark 6.31).*

We too can be recharged, re-energized and refocused, by returning to base and taking time out with our Father.

Charging complete ...

What a lovely thought! When our charging is complete, we are ready to face anything!

Extract taken from Liz Babbs, *Into God's Presence – Listening to God through prayer and meditation* (Zondervan 2005).

O God,
be all my love,
all my hope,
all my striving;
let my thoughts and words flow from you,
my daily life be in you,
and every breath I take be for you.

John Cassian

When we speak with God, our power of addressing him, of holding communion with him, and listening to his still, small voice, depends upon our will being one and the same with his.

Florence Nightingale

To worship God in spirit and truth means to worship God as we ought to worship him. God is Spirit, so we must worship him in spirit and truth, that is, by a humble and true adoration of spirit in the depth and centre of our souls. God alone can see this worship; we can repeat it so often that in the end it becomes as if it were natural to us, and as if God were one with our souls, and our souls one with him.

Brother Lawrence

Get your perspective restored day after day. He is God and you belong to him. Everything else is secondary to that wonderful fact. Let it grip you, flood your heart. Leap down the street in its joy. The Lord is God. The Lord is God! And we belong to him.

Michael Baughen

೮೦ ೮ಽ ೮೦

It is when the love of God is allowed to penetrate every corner of a person's being that the peace of God comes as a positive gift, as a sturdy guardian of the soul's inward rest. The sharing of anxieties and fears, this intimate thankfulness for joy and beauty, brings the individual very close to the life of God. It must be habitual and it must be practised, but its fruit is a relaxed spirit.

J.B. Phillips

೮೦ ೮ಽ ೮೦

God ... is longing for a time of communion with His children. Specifically, He longs to meet with you. He knows you know that He loves you. But still, He wants to say it again. He knows you know that He is faithful, but He wants to show His faithfulness once again.

Anonymous

May the mind of Christ my Saviour
Live in me from day to day,
By his love and power controlling
All I do and say.

May the word of God dwell richly
In my heart from hour to hour,
So that all may see I triumph
Only through his power.

Kate Wilkinson

୫୦ ୪ ୫୦

The essence of prayer does not consist in asking God for something but in opening our hearts to God, in speaking with him, and living with him in perpetual communion. Prayer is continual abandonment to God. Prayer does not mean asking God for all kinds of things we want; it is rather the desire for God himself, the only giver of life. Prayer is not asking, but union with God. Prayer is not a painful effort to gain from God help in the varying needs of our lives. Prayer is the desire to possess God himself, the source of all life. The true spirit of prayer does not consist in asking for blessings, but in receiving Him who is the giver of all blessings, and in living a life of fellowship with him.

Sadhu Sundar Singh

Prayer

The human heart is a silent harp in God's choir, whose strings need only to be swept by the divine breath to chime in with the harmonies of creation.

Henry David Thoreau

Lord Jesus Christ,
fill us, we pray, with your light,
that we may reflect your wondrous glory.
So fill us with your love,
that we may count nothing too small to do
   for you,
nothing too much to give,
and nothing too hard to bear.

Anonymous

You know the value of prayer; it is precious beyond all price. Never, never neglect it.

Thomas Buxton

Praying the Psalms

Robert Dolman

Dietrich Bonhoeffer subtitled his book about the Psalms, 'The Prayer Book of the Bible'.[1] When we say the Psalms we are caught up in the prayer ceaselessly offered by the multitude of believers through the ages. We tune our instruments and play our part in the perpetual symphony of the liturgy of the Church, and our private prayers are delivered from their parochialism and isolation.

These resilient texts form an inexhaustible treasury of spiritual wisdom. They are still amazingly accessible to us, speaking with an authentic voice in our contemporary world. They are studded with richly rewarding images of God and other nourishing metaphors and phrases. They are a 'primary technology for developing a life of prayer'.[2] When we use them regularly and know them by heart, they inform all our praying, both formal acts of devotion and spontaneous 'arrow prayers' of love. They bring to our spirituality the dimensions of unfettered praise, of sheer exuberant delight in God's merciful goodness and providential care and of celebration of the generous bounty of the earth. Their joyful words fall like refreshing rain in the dry and thirsty places of our lives.

The Psalms are, of course, creative poetry. Poetry is often the
best medium in which to express the transcendant because it
slows us down and makes us brood and ponder. 'Poetry grabs
for the jugular. Far from being cosmetic language, it is
intestinal.'[3] If we carry the Psalms with us in our hearts, they
can lead us from the shallows of conventional piety into the
depths of contemplation. Melvyn Matthews writes:

> Nowhere else in the Scriptures do you come
> nearer to the very glory or 'presence' of the
> Lord. As you read them you know that the
> Psalms both create and fill our 'Godspace'
> until your heart breaks for joy. There is
> nothing the contemplative person wants
> more than the opportunity to pray the
> Psalms slowly and in silence, because they
> know that in so doing they are brought
> before the face of God in praise and in
> thanksgiving, in supplication and in
> adoration, as by nothing else.[4]

The Psalms are the voice of common humanity, reflecting the
sum total of our experience of God, the polar opposites of awe
and intimacy, of serene trust and disillusioned despair. Real
prayer has to engage candidly with the whole of life, and with
the agonies of doubt and pain in a broken and unjust world,
rather than just echo our romantic feelings. Lavinia Byrne
writes, 'There was a terrible movement about ten years ago to
produce a sanitised version of the Psalms, where all the ugly,
angry bits got left out, and God was all sweetness and light. It

is terribly difficult to come to God genuinely in prayer if you have to be benign.'[5] Gordon Rupp wrote that the Psalms strike notes, which are silent on most of our English spiritual pianos.[6] Meditating on the Psalms, especially the verses we find difficult, enables us to deal constructively with the negative emotions that flood into our own hearts and minds and the self-pity and the ugly and unresolved aspects of ourselves which we, arrayed in our Sunday best, are disposed to repress and disown. The Psalms are prayers of the whole person.

As many as 40 of the Psalms may be classified as 'psalms of lament'. Recent commentators have stressed their importance for balanced Christian devotion and regretted their neglect. Too often a facile spirituality creates the impression that Christians are always successful and at peace. Unaffected by life's ills and disasters, they cuddle up to their God who serves simply as a child's undemanding, faithful comforter. The Psalms insist that we face in our prayer lives both the sufferings of the world and the God of righteousness and justice who is seeking to destroy the agents of darkness. It is true that there are some Psalms that we may not want to use in public worship but their hostility to the enemies of God's kingdom, even when it takes the form of cursing, may have a significant place within our personal reflection. 'The crucified Jesus teaches us to pray the imprecatory psalms correctly.'[7]

When we pray the Psalms, then, we join in the prayer of the whole Church, expressing its penitence, its sorrows and joys and its yearning for God. They articulate for us the petitions of our voiceless and oppressed sisters and brothers who, in the midst of their traumatic struggles, have asked us to pray on their behalf. 'So when we are thrilled by good news and yet find ourselves complaining with the psalmist that God seems far from us and that our enemies surround us, we are praying for the elderly widow in a high-rise block who is afraid of the drug pushers outside her door, or the person who feels abandoned by God as they watch a loved one dying in hospital.'[8] The language of savage protest and tearful complaint may be the only prayer that many people, and perhaps especially those normally outside the worshipping community, can with integrity make their own. So the whole amount of human emotion is laid in the presence of God, 'like a golden retriever bringing to its master's feet every strange object it can find in the field'.[9]

'Being able to tell God that I hate someone is quite revolutionary for me.'[10] 'It is an act of profound faith to entrust one's most precious hatreds to God, knowing they will be taken seriously.'[11] By helping us to acknowledge the vengeful and malicious thoughts we prefer not to have, reciting the Psalms can absolve us from our darker moods and release us to sing to the Lord a new song. Walter Brueggemann traces the way in which psalms which reflect the chaotic 'disorientation' that constantly dogs our lives give way to the psalms of 'new orientation' and their 'extravagant summons to praise'.[12] Hymns or worship songs, by contrast, with their lofty, triumphalist sentiments, seldom allow us to start from where we really are. For this reason the tendency to replace psalms with hymns in private devotions needs to be resisted. Not many hymns, even those modelled on the Psalms, express as honestly as the Psalms themselves the dialogue between faith and doubt, between our higher aspirations and our urgent questioning. 'There is an old Jewish prescription for help in time of trouble: drink a warm glass of milk and read the Psalms, beginning at the beginning and taking them as they come.'[13]

If to read the whole of the Psalter is to pray as a whole person with the whole Church, it is also to pray with Jesus. His growing mind was saturated with these verses, and they shed light on his ministry. We need to remember too that the Psalms bear witness to him, as much as do the Law and the Prophets. In the setting of the Christian liturgy, celebrating the saving activity of God in Jesus Christ, the Psalms find a new resonance and yield rich insights into his mystery. 'The Psalms are given to us to this end, that we may learn to pray in the name of Jesus Christ.'[14]

Notes

1. Dietrich Bonhoeffer, *The Psalms, the Prayer Book of the Bible,* Augsburg Publishing House, 1974.
2. Eugene H. Peterson, *Answering God, Learning to Pray from the Psalms,* Marshall Pickering, 1989, p. 6.
3. Eugene H. Peterson, *Answering God, Learning to Pray from the Psalms,* p. 11.
4. Melvyn Matthews, *God's Space in You,* Hunt and Thorpe, 1992, p. 48.

5. Lavinia Byrne, *The Journey is My Home*, Hodder and Stoughton, 2000, p. 165.

6. *Methodist Recorder*, 29 May 1986.

7. Dietrich Bonhoeffer, *The Psalms, the Prayer Book of the Bible,* p. 60.

8. Christopher Cocksworth and Rosalind Brown, *Being a Priest Today*, Canterbury Press, 2002, p. 113.

9. Tom Wright, *Simply Christian*, SPCK, 2006, p. 130.

10. Eugene H. Peterson, *Answering God, Learning to Pray from the Psalms,* p. 133.

11. Walter Brueggemann, *The Message of the Psalms*, Augsburg Publishing House, 1984, p. 77.

12. Walter Brueggemann, *The Message of the Psalms*, p. 77.

13. Bernhard Anderson, *Out of the Depths: the Psalms speak for us today*, Westminster Knox Press, 3rd edition, 2000, p. 210.

14. Dietrich Bonhoeffer, *The Psalms, the Prayer Book of the Bible,* p. 15.

Praying the Psalms

O God, you are my God; eagerly I seek you,
My soul thirsts for you, my flesh faints for you
As in a barren and dry land where there is no water

Therefore I have gazed upon you in your holy place.
That I might behold your power and your glory.

For your loving-kindness is better than life itself;
My lips shall give you praise.

So I will bless you as long as I live
And lift up my hands in your name.

Psalm 63

ജ   ഇ   ജ

*If ... our worship is true to the totality of its Judeo-Christian
inheritance, it will not be all bright and clear, thin in colour,
humanistic and this-world in telling. It will retain the ancient
sense of cloud and darkness, other-worldly fire and light,
which still lives in the Psalter; the awe before a sacred
mystery which is with us and yet never of us, the deep sense
of imperfection, and above all the unconquerable trust and
the adoring love for a God who has set his glory above the
heavens and yet is mindful of the children of men.*

Evelyn Underhill

Prayer

With sandals off, then, and imagination at the ready, you begin to read a psalm. Don't look for logic. The writer is not a scientist, at pains to watch every syllable he writes lest he get a fact wrong. Here are people in agony. Here are people exuberant. Here are people at moments of high spiritual experience. Don't look for logic. Rather, listen for a heartbeat. And remember that you are in the world of poetry – these psalms are *poems*, and poems need *time* ...

Donald Coggan

Not all psalms are the same. Some of them are majestic hymns of praise to God, reflecting the joy of the jubilant worshipper, who is at peace with God and with the world. By contrast, others reflect the darker moments of human experience. Sometimes the worshipper recognised his or her own guilt as the cause of the trouble. But on other occasions the worshipper protests that he is truly innocent, and ought not to be suffering in the first place. Such emotions are familiar to us all, for they are part and parcel of life in every place and at every time.

John Drane

There is one thing still remaining which cannot be neglected without great injury to your devotions, to begin all your prayers with a psalm. There is nothing that so clears a way for your prayers, nothing that so disperses dullness of heart, nothing that so purifies the soul from poor and little passions, nothing so opens heaven or carries your heart so near it as these songs of praise.

William Law

ℬ   ℭ   ℬ

Do you sometimes feel like the Psalmist and cry 'out of the depths'? He prays for God to hear and be merciful. He takes comfort in God's forgiveness. He is prepared to wait for the Lord and hope in his word. It seems he had problems like all of us!

Cyril Skerratt

ℬ   ℭ   ℬ

The psalms live on because they reflect a profound belief in a God who had done wonderful things in the past, for which he should be praised and held in awe ... a God who, despite the distresses and difficulties of those who called upon him, could be trusted to ensure justice in the future. ... The psalms convey emotions that can often resonate with those of the modern reader.

Adrian Curtis

Prayer

There is no relationship more striking than
the way the Psalmists speak of God, and
speak to God. Not all are ... on their way to a
religious festival. Some are toilers like
ourselves, trudging at times ways difficult
and drear. Some are of the city with its
crowds; some of the country with its hills,
trees and patchwork plain. Some go down to
the sea in ships, and do business in the great
waters. But wherever life finds them, day in,
day out, their song rises vibrant with life.

Rita Snowden

In verses 19-22 [of Psalm 103] the psalmist catches a glimpse
of the worship of the LORD, the King of heaven. Worshipping
in the temple, he finds himself caught up into the very
worship of heaven itself, with his voice added to those of
'angels, archangels and all the company of heaven'.
Experiences like this are not common in the Bible, nor do they
happen very often in our lives today, but, when they do occur,
they put us in touch with something higher, deeper and richer,
and provide another way in which the response of 'praise' is
generated in us.

Stephen B. Dawes

'Preserve us, Lord'

Deborah Smith Douglas

Before I get out of bed most days, I (sleepily and silently) say this short traditional collect from the Anglican Prayer Book's form of morning prayer:

> Lord God, almighty and everlasting Father, you have brought us in safety to this new day: Preserve us with your mighty power, that we may not fall into sin, nor be overcome by adversity; and in all we do, direct us to the fulfilling of your purpose, through Jesus Christ our Lord. Amen.

Recently, to my dismay, whenever I say the phrase 'preserve us', an incongruous image springs irresistibly to mind: my grandmothers' fruit cellar. Row on gleaming row of bottled plums, spiced peaches, chutney, green beans and tomatoes and corn, strawberry jam and grape jelly, glowing like jewels in the light of the single electric bulb in the ceiling.

This involuntary linking of the petition to 'preserve us' with a memory of jam jars in a basement was mortifying. How frivolous of my unruly brain, I thought, to intrude a kind of visual pun on my waking prayer: how irreverent and irrelevant. But the more I tried to avoid the association the more persistent it became. So I began to wonder what it might mean. And as I rummaged in my mind for the connection, I have come to see that it is neither irrelevant nor irreverent at all.

When as a child I was sent down to the fruit cellar to fetch cherry jam for breakfast or runner beans for supper, my admiration for the beauty and order of the packed rows of jars was grounded in personal knowledge of the huge labour that had gone into them. A whole summer had been salvaged; an entire harvest rescued from worm and frost and weed and waste, in long days in garden and kitchen.

To my young eye, the preparations for a canning day were awesome in their ritual severity: the grandmothers wrapped in spotless aprons, the kitchen table scrubbed to whiteness, the glass jars sterilized to a surgical standard, timers checked, knives sharpened, the sacrifice itself (whatever was perfectly ripe that week) scrutinized, selected, washed, prepared. Unassuming Lutheran women were suddenly vested with the gravity and assurance of priests; lifting dripping racks of sterile jars from clouds of steam, stirring kettles, judiciously adding salt and vinegar and sugar, finally filling the jars and sealing them.

But what has this to do with prayer?

The word 'preserve' itself, of course, is key. To preserve means to save – to keep safe from harm, to rescue from destruction. The 'saving' of fruits and vegetables that the grandmothers (like countless women before them) undertook each summer fed the family all winter: it was important work, demanding skill and risk and patience. For all its no-nonsense practical seriousness, it was also – indeed primarily – an act of love: love not as something wonderful we feel but something difficult we do.

All of this, I realize now, lies just below the surface of that involuntary linking of my adult prayer and my childhood memory.

Thanking God for bringing us safely to a new day – asking him to 'preserve' us from sin and adversity that we may be useful to his purpose – reveals the whole labour-intensive love-infused enterprise stored up in my grandmothers' fruit cellar to be an apt and powerful image of the saving love of God.

In the first place, the comparison reminds us that we do not save ourselves, any more than the produce of my grandmothers' garden made its own way into kettle and jar. It is only God's steadfast love and faithfulness that 'continually preserve' us (Psalm 40.11 KJV); the Lord alone will deliver us from evil and 'preserve [us] unto his heavenly kingdom' (2 Timothy 4.18 KJV). It is utterly beyond our power to achieve our own salvation.

At the same time, we are in urgent need of being saved. If we stay as we are, we will have been planted and tended in vain, forfeit to death, as surely as the tomatoes in my grandmothers' garden would have rotted if they had been left on the vine. My grandmothers kept their garden watered and weeded and safe from harm not for the benefit of marauding rabbits or for the plants' own pleasure, but to fulfil their own sustaining purposes: to feed their family and neighbours.

So it is with us. The purpose of human life (as the Westminster Catechism puts it) is 'to glorify God and enjoy him forever' – not, contrary to the assumptions of popular culture, to glorify or enjoy ourselves. As Evelyn Underhill once rather tartly reminded a friend (who seems to have been unhappily preoccupied with her own imperfections), 'The object of your salvation is God's glory, not your happiness.' Enlarging the agricultural metaphor, C.S. Lewis suggests that 'we are like eggs at present', and we cannot go on indefinitely just being eggs: 'We must be hatched or go bad.'

The salvation unto eternal life that God intends for us will involve our being radically changed: 'hatched' like eggs, plucked like fruit from the orchard, dying to one nature that we might be born to another. Jesus reminds us that only if a grain of wheat falls into the earth and dies, will it bear fruit (John 12.24). And if that wheat is not harvested – cut and winnowed and ground – of what value is its life? When we ask God to 'preserve us' from sin and adversity that we might fulfil his purpose for our lives, we are asking God to transform us and use us: as wheat is changed to bread and grapes to wine.

Unlike the produce of my grandmothers' garden, plucked and peeled and boiled and strained without its knowledge or consent, we are privileged to participate in our own transformation. By the grace of God, we may (and in this morning prayer we do) say an ever-deeper yes to God's 'mighty power' and mysterious purposes. We may – in fact we must – continuously offer ourselves to whatever discipline and suffering that regeneration and sanctification will require. Cardinal Newman, knowing that he must be transformed if he hoped to see God, prayed: 'O support me as I proceed in this great, awful, happy change.'

Our incarnate, crucified and risen Lord does indeed support us as we surrender to being made new, part of the 'new creation' (2 Corinthians 5.17). Christ himself sets us free from our bondage to decay (Romans 8.21). By his death and resurrection, he is both the model for perfect obedience and trust in God, even unto death, and the means by which we too can hope to enjoy God for ever, and participate in the saving of the world God loves.

These are great matters, almost too much to grasp, a prospect of glory that dazzles us.

Perhaps that is why my grandmothers' fruit cellar has become for me, in all its rootedness in domestic 'ordinary time', a consoling image of the household of God: rank on rank of the 'preserved', the rescued, changed from one nature to another by means of water and fire, set apart in love for the sustaining of the family, the neighbourhood, the world.

Prayer

O God the Creator and Sustainer of the world, who provides sufficient food for our need but not for our greed, bless your wild creation so that it yields a rich harvest for all your dependent creatures, and sufficient for our needs; and give us such a feeling of gratefulness that we do not spoil their environment nor their harvest.

Give us generous hearts to recognize the needs of others, and open our hands to help, knowing that in others we see they eyes of our Lord and Saviour Jesus Christ.

Prayer for Harvest

When life is seen as the gift of God praise and thanksgiving is inevitable. When reverence and respect for the material world, for the earth itself, for the mundane activities of daily life, are a natural part of life, then there can never be any denigration of matter itself. The generosity of God in sharing the goodness of creation with us can elicit only one possible response – that of gratitude.

Esther de Waal

Every act from a life lived in good relationship with the Creator, and extended to all of creation, is a prayer. In my steps, my work, preparing my food, or creating something of beauty, there is an element of prayer, an acknowledgement of touching God, and knowing that God is touching me.

Ray Buckley

'Preserve us, Lord'

One of the main purposes of meditation is to expose us to the reality of the Father in such a way that we can become the kind of people who are able to love. His life radiating through us cleanses, heals and transforms us. Then we can truly love in the way that Jesus asked of us. He did not tell us that we are his followers when we are great at meditating and religious activities, but only when we love one another as he loved us. This is the ultimate criterion of our lives, which can be fully realized only as we turn inward and open ourselves to God.

Morton T. Kelsey

All this day, O Lord,
let me touch as many lives as possible for thee;
and every life I touch, do thou by thy Spirit quicken,
whether through the word I speak,
the prayer I breathe, or the life I live.

Mary Sumner

In worship we behold the goodness of God, and become partakers of that goodness; in worship we see the patience of God, and become partakers of that patience; we celebrate the purpose of God, and offer ourselves as servants of that purpose.

Nels Ferré

But what if I
should hear that voice
practical,
earthy,
specific,
speaking to me?

What if God should say,
'I have heard,
I will save,
now you must hear
and go
and be the instrument of my salvation'?

I want to stand
and see the glory of God,
to wonder,
to worship
and be still ...
but what if God says 'Go!'?

Edmund Banyard

ॐ   ॐ   ॐ

*It was to me a great discovery when I passed from the
thought of doing work and asking God to help me to do it, to
the faith that God is doing work, and the prayer that he
would let me help him to do it.*

Father Andrew

We do not pray, of course, simply because it does us good; balanced prayer embraces worship and thanksgiving to God and intercession for others as well as personal petition. Nonetheless we are clearly encouraged to come frequently to God and beseech his help and blessing in face of the challenge to live for him and serve him in the world.

Bruce Milne

Give me an open ear, O God, that I may hear thy voice
calling me to high endeavour.
Give me an open mind, O God, a mind ready to receive and to
welcome such new light of knowledge as it is thy will to reveal
to me.
Give me open eyes, O God, eyes quick to discover
thine indwelling in the world which Thou hast made.
Give me open hands, O God, hands ready to share with all
who are in want
the blessings with which thou hast enriched my life.

John Baillie

ಬ   ೧

No network signal

Lorna Lackenby

Prayer,
an open channel of communication;
no out of range,
no peak rate tariff,
no credit running low,
no price per text.
These things I know
and yet,
somehow,
I back myself into a corner
of 'no network signal'.

Prayer,
I know what I want to say;
but I get distracted,
my mind wanders,
my diary gets full,
other things crowd in.
I start with good intentions
and yet,
somehow,
I drift into an apathetic abyss
of 'no network signal'.

Prayer,
Sometimes I don't know how to communicate;
I'm angry and hurt,
want to shout, even rant,
my inner child screams,
'It's not fair!'
I try to find a way to start
and yet,
somehow,
lacking honesty, I plunge to a place
of 'no network signal'.

Prayer,
I'm sure that is has become part of my life;
I pray at Church,
When I'm in crisis,
if something 'wows' me,
for strength when I'm weary,
I pray because I do
and yet,
somehow,
I stagnate, stumbling into a habit
of 'no network signal'.

Prayer,
an open channel of communication;
limited only by me,
paid for by Christ,
networked by the Holy Spirit,
to give free Parental conversation.
These things I know
and so,
in new strength,
I am released, find full signal,
for I am ready to allow a reply.

No network signal

Thanx 4 stickin wiv me God even tho I
not gr8 @ prayin. Pls help me 2 keep
in touch so I can follow ur way & not
get lost. Til l8r Lord, Amen.

*Accept me, O Lord, just as I am, in my frailty and
inadequacy, contradictions, confusions and complexities,
with all those discordant currents that pull me in so many
directions.*

*Accept all of this and help me so to live with what I am that
what I am may become my way to God.*

*Accept the tensions and help me to hold them together, so
that I may learn to live fully, freely, wholly, not torn apart
but finding that balance and harmony that will allow me to
discover my point of inner equilibrium.*

Source unknown

The fruit that silence brings is known to them who have
experienced it. God has led us into solitude to speak to our
heart.

St Bruno

Prayer

We all go through periods of dryness in our prayers, don't we? ... I sometimes suspect that what we feel to be our best prayers are really our worst; that what we are enjoying is the satisfaction of apparent success, as in executing a dance or reciting a poem. Do our prayers sometimes go wrong because we insist on trying to talk to God when he wants to talk to us?

C.S. Lewis

Prayer is not asking. It is a longing of the soul. It is daily admission of one's weakness. It is better in prayer to have a heart without words than words without a heart.

Mahatma Gandhi

First, give God a chance. Take your problem, whatever it may be, to him in prayer. Tell him all about it – just as if he didn't know a thing. In the telling be absolutely honest and sincere. Hold nothing back. ... Then the second step is to believe that God will hear you. Remember that he heard the poor woman who only touched the hem of his garment. Believe with all your faith that he cares what happens to you. You must believe that. You can't doubt it when you look at the cross. Next, you must wait patiently for the Lord. He does not answer every prayer on Sunday afternoon! ... But wait. God is never in a hurry.

Peter Marshall

Lord, I believe in you, help my unbelief.
I love you, yet not with a perfect heart as I would.
I long for you, yet not with my full strength.
I trust in you, yet not with my whole mind.
Accept my faith, my love, my longing to know and
    serve you, my trust in your power to keep me.
I wait your blessing.
Through Christ my Lord.

Malcolm Spencer

ᏠᎠ   ᏟᎹ   ᏠᎠ

There are whole periods when you are neither at the bottom of
the sea nor at the top of the peak, when you have to do
something about praying, and that is the period when you
cannot pray from spontaneity but you can pray from
conviction.

Anthony Bloom

ᏠᎠ   ᏟᎹ   ᏠᎠ

Just for today, what does it matter, O Lord,
    if the future is dark?
To pray for tomorrow I am not able. Keep
    my heart only for today, grant me your
    light, just for today.

Thérèse of Lisieux

Her first tentative efforts to pray again ... had been hard at first. ... But she persevered, giving her worthlessness bravely into the hands of God, and gradually all the old power had come back. Only it had come back with a difference. In the old days she had felt as though the laughter and strength that she brought away from her hours of prayer had flowed out from herself; now she knew that they flowed only through her, and what delighted her was the miraculous power of God that could pick up even an empty straw and make it the channel of his grace.

Elizabeth Goudge

If we knew how to listen to God, we should hear him speaking to us. For God does speak. He speaks in his Gospel; he speaks also through life – the new Gospel to which we ourselves add a page each day.

Michel Quoist

It is not enough to begin to pray, nor to pray aright; nor is it enough to continue for a time to pray, but we must patiently, believingly, continue in prayer unto the end; and further we have not only to continue in prayer ... but we have also to believe that God does hear us, and will answer our prayer.

George Muller

Thinking about prayer

Ann Lewin

'Have you done your practice? Have you said your prayers?'

Those are two questions I remember from my childhood. Odd questions ... no one in the house could have failed to notice whether I had done my practice. And my mother was always in the house. The other question seemed a bit intrusive. Whether I'd said my prayers or not seemed to be my affair, not anyone else's. But my discomfort at being asked the question arose more from the fact that on the occasion I remember, I had to say 'no'. And I got the distinct impression that that was the wrong answer!

Reflecting later, I realized that these were not really questions at all, but a bit of parental control, making sure that I did the important things – rather like 'Have you cleaned your teeth?' And further reflection, much later on, made me think that *as* questions, they entirely missed the point. Doing my practice, saying my prayers were not activities for their own sake, to be done, ticked off for the day and then forgotten about until the next parental nudge; they both led on to something greater. Piano practice was important because it was part of becoming more musical – something those within earshot must have hoped would happen sooner, rather than later. And saying my prayers was part of growing more prayerful, part of establishing that relationship with God which is the foundation of all Christian living. I wonder if it would have been more helpful if I had been asked 'Have you become more musical today? Have you become more prayerful?'

Prayer is an expression of our relationship with God – and one of the other things about it that I eventually realized is that *saying* my prayers, like practising scales, was only the beginning: my practice needed to spill over into the whole of my life. Because that is what relationships are like. We don't stop being related when we are not consciously present with the person with whom we are in relationship. The relationship continues as we go about the ordinary things of life. We may think of the person we relate to from time to time – 'John would be interested in this; I must remember to tell Mary'.... And from time to time, regularly, we need time with the other person to catch up, get to know them better, enjoy their company. I know that I don't play the piano nearly as well now that I don't practise. We all know of relationships that drift or founder because we don't make time for them.

So our prayer time is the time when we practise the presence of God, so that *all* our life may be filled with the presence of God. Most people think that behaviour matters and prayer helps it. The truth is that prayer matters, and behaviour tests it.[1]

One of the odd things about our Christian life is that on the whole we don't talk about prayer. I had piano lessons which didn't just test how I was getting on, but gave me and the teacher a chance to look at techniques that would help – a difficult passage would become easier to cope with if I sorted the fingering out, or a piece of music might come to life if I played some of it more quietly, and didn't just hit the notes .... But I didn't have much help with learning to pray. It was something that on the whole I was left to get on with. We went to church, there was the odd sermon, but I don't remember anyone saying to me, 'How are you getting on with your prayer life?' So I suppose I grew up thinking that I was supposed to know about prayer, and that everyone else already knew. That is what we do think, probably. We look around and see everyone else devoutly concentrating, and don't realize that behind the closed eyes and clasped hands, there is as much confusion and inattention as there is in us.

There is a skit by Joyce Grenfell in which she is shown in church singing a hymn: 'Calm and untroubled are my thoughts' – and then we realize that she is singing what she is actually thinking about – she forgot to turn the gas down under the saucepan of chicken bones she was turning into stock; she imagines the pan boiling dry, the stove, then the house, catching fire; where will they sleep tonight? If she goes home now, she might be in time to save the picture which is supposed to be a Picasso, though she'd much rather save her photograph album .... She turns to her husband and sings, 'I suppose you didn't think to check the gas? No, I didn't think you would have.' The skit ends with her singing again, 'Calm and untroubled are my thoughts'.

It's funny not just because it's Joyce Grenfell, but because it rings true for us all. We all find it difficult to concentrate, to find time – we get stuck in ways of praying that perhaps we need to grow on from. We have to learn to move from having a time of prayer to having a life of prayer. That takes practice. Unlike the piano practice, there are no exams – we're not going to be better than the people who've only passed Grade III. The aim is not to be 'good' at prayer – I don't know what that would mean – but to be faithful in establishing the prayerfulness of the whole of life. There is nothing that can't be prayerful. If we can think of anything that can't be prayerful, perhaps we need to question whether we should be doing it at all.

Nothing that can't be prayerful. There's the story of two monks who argued about whether you could drink coffee and pray at the same time. They couldn't agree, so they went off to ask their spiritual directors for advice. When they came back, they still couldn't agree. One monk said, 'My director said, "No, on no account must you let anything interfere with prayer."' The other monk said, 'That's odd, my director didn't think there was a problem at all. What did you ask?'

The first monk said, 'I asked if I could drink coffee while I was praying, and my director got quite cross with me.'

The other laughed. 'Oh, I asked whether I could pray while I was drinking coffee.'

It's all about changing our attitudes, about growing into a deeper understanding. What we are about is coming closer to the God who loves us – and our response to that love can be expressed in the words of Julian of Norwich, that wise woman from the fourteenth century. She prayed, 'God, of your goodness give us yourself; for if we ask anything that is less, we shall always be in want. Only in you we have all.'[2]

Notes

1. After William Temple, 'The proper relation in thought between prayer and conduct is not that conduct is supremely important and prayer may help it, but that prayer is supremely important, and conduct tests it.'
    From *Christus Veritas*, published Macmillan, London 1924. Quoted by Gordon Mursell in *English Spirituality: From 1700 to the Present Day, vol. 2, p. 373*, SPCK.

2. *Revelation of Divine Love*, Long Text ch. 5.

Extract taken from Ann Lewin, *Words by the Way*, (Inspire 2005).

Prayer

Almighty God,
give us wisdom to perceive you,
wisdom to understand you,
diligence to seek you,
patience to wait for you,
eyes to behold you,
a heart to meditate upon you,
and life to proclaim you,
through the power of the Spirit
of our Lord, Jesus Christ. Amen.

St Benedict

Live in peace yourself, and then
you can bring peace to others.

Thomas à Kempis

What God desires is that we should share life with him. He is, as we profess to believe, always at hand, concerned in all our concerns, ever responsive to our call. It should become an easy and natural thing to recollect and act upon this at any moment. There is no mood or condition of mind which he does not understand. There is no experience or encounter in which he has not something to say to us, something to give us.

Philip J. Fisher

Prayer is co-operation with God. It is the purest exercise of the faculties God has given us, an exercise that links these faculties with the Maker to work out the intentions he has in mind in their creation.

E. Stanley Jones

℞ ℗ ℞

I think I want a more familiar God whom I can turn to at any minute of the day without fear, rather than a Being who must be approached with extra special language on one's knees, or by priests in special vestments. It is everything not only to reverence him but to love him, and to feel that you know him so well that you can even enjoy fun with him.

Edward Wilson

℞ ℗ ℞

Prayer at its highest is a two-way conversation, and for me the most important part is listening to God's replies.

Frank C. Laubach

Prayer

Communication with God – prayer – is a two-way conversation! It is not just the voice of praise and petitions, but often communion. Sitting in silence with God, listening for whatever He may want to say. Simply enjoy the fact that He is, and you are, and you have a relationship with Him. These special moments with God are when His fresh breezes can enter your heart and refresh you.

Anonymous

Pray as you can, and do not try to pray as you can't.

John Chapman

Prayer is not merely claiming a hearing, it is giving a hearing. It is not only speaking to God; it is listening to God. And as the heavens are higher than the earth, so are the words we hear greater than the words we speak. ... [God's] word comes downward into our lives laden with the quiet certainty of the Eternal, wide as the vision of God who sees all, deep as the wisdom of God who knows all. So however much it may be to say 'Hear me', it is vastly more to say, 'Cause me to hear.'

Percy Ainsworth (adapted)

Drop Thy still dews of quietness,
Till all our strivings cease;
Take from our souls the strain and stress,
And let our ordered lives confess
The beauty of Thy peace.

Breathe through the heats of our desire
Thy coolness and Thy balm;
Let sense be dumb, let flesh retire;
Speak through the earthquake, wind, and fire,
O still, small voice of calm.

John Greenleaf Whittier

      ß‿   ɞ   ßɔ

When we pray aright, we shall be concerned that things are not so much *for* us as *to* us. We shall be seeking not just gifts but the Giver ... We shall no longer be concerned to get what *we* want, but to discover what God wants. We shall come not just with open hands, but with open hearts; not only to receive but to give.

David N. Francis

The pilgrimage of prayer

Frank Collier

A friend once commented that in praying for other people we are nearer to the heart of God than at any other time. I have grown to share that conviction. I am deeply disappointed when, during a service, a preacher omits intercessions or offers them in a perfunctory fashion. It seems as though the expression of Christian love in worship has only been half fulfilled.

Intercession is essential to our response to God. We want to share his love with others. I have seen this in a village Methodist church every Sunday morning. At the very outset the lay assistant tells the congregation about the suffering and the deep concerns of the village people, and about the joys which have been theirs. People who do not share the Christian faith are still brought to God in a loving prayer. It is one of the most inspiring moments when occasionally I visit that village as a preacher. It points to a wonderful depth in the life of that church.

Even in the ordinary intercessions of a church a preacher can try to identify both the joys and the needs of those around him. So he or she might pray:

For all beset by pain or hopelessness.
For children in unhappy homes or disabled in mind or body.
For those who have lost the ability to love.
For the desperately ill and the old who are forgotten.
For those who lack the faith to find forgiveness and are dogged by an uneasy conscience.

There must be many who need these prayers.

I woke up to the importance of these prayers when reading St Thomas à Kempis:

I offer up to thee all the pious desires of devout persons, the necessities of parents, friends, brethren and sisters and all those who have done good to me and to others for thy love.

He also prayed for people who had hurt him or whom he himself had hurt. He was very near to the heart of God.

I had the beginnings of a concern for intercession when at 18 I was greatly privileged to hear a four-year-old girl saying her prayers. Her concluding words were quite startling: 'Please, God, bless those people I don't like.' Twelve years later I visited a church in a very difficult housing estate where women of the church and the neighbourhood visited a very caring woman of very limited education, seeking her prayers. Her prayers were wonderfully effective.

We need, of course, to find the pattern of our prayers in the prayers of Jesus himself. There is a hint for us in the words of Jesus to Peter just before the crucifixion. He told Peter that he had prayed for him that his strength would not fail, and he laid upon him the responsibility of strengthening his fellow disciples.

In St John's Gospel there is a very illuminating prayer. It shows that Jesus recognized the trials that would face the disciples. He will not be there to protect them but he prays for their protection. Perhaps here is a pattern for us when people we love face great trials but are out of reach of our personal help. We must do what is within our reach first of all. What is noticeable is that Jesus does not pray for his disciples to be taken out of danger, but rather protected from what might corrupt their spirits.

Jesus also prays that his disciples will receive the Holy Spirit. Here is the sustaining strength for preaching, teaching and healing. But it could also include gifts which Paul has called the harvest of the Spirit. They consist of love, joy, peace, patience, kindness, goodness, faithfulness, gentleness and self-control. Here too is a pattern for our prayers of intercession for those we love.

Prayer today involves problems for many people, especially for the young. H.E. Fosdick pointed out the problems created by scientific discovery:

The world looks like a great machine, self-running and self-regulating, with God a very distant sustainer.

That problem has grown more acute in the last 40 years. In the 1960s a Christian head teacher could invite a local minister to his morning assembly. I heard very moving addresses on the sufferings of the disabled and one short talk about the sufferings of the people of an Indian village. The youngsters were socially a very mixed community but they would respond with their prayers and would want to talk about the problems afterwards. Today many youngsters cannot often believe that any God is concerned with the teeming millions of our planet. So it is much more difficult to persuade young people to pray. Perhaps a terrifying world disaster or the suffering of someone they greatly love may move them to pray, but it is not easy for them.

Nor is that the only problem. Christians have always been bewildered when a quite unselfish prayer remains unanswered. Men and women will blame themselves for not praying properly, or they will search for sin which they have committed. Unhappily they sometimes lose their faith, though actually no word of Jesus ever suggested that God does not answer prayers because we are sinful. Apparently unanswered prayer for those we love and even for the needy people of the world remains a pressing problem for many sincere Christian people.

Another difficulty occurs when, imperceptibly, we want God to enforce our will on somebody very near to us. We believe that we are praying for their good, that what we want is the best way for them. Sometimes we are near to the truth and our prayer is an expression of love, but unhappily we are too often wanting our own way. Indeed, we are often most selfish when praying for people in our own family. Perhaps it is all the more important that we dwell often on the great prayers of Christians down the centuries, and that can help us to be truly unselfish.

I write this because I have found that intercession has strengthened my own fellowship with God. In my early thirties a personal crisis left me unable to pray. Then one Sunday I worshipped under the guidance of the Revd Leslie Weatherhead. He described the desperate needs of four suffering people and asked us to pray for them in a time of quiet. I was moved to pray for them and suddenly found that I could pray for myself. The door had seemed closed but that moment of compassion had brought me back to God. It had also pointed out a pattern of prayer that has shaped my prayers ever since. The discovery was momentous. When a gleam of unselfish love enters our hearts we have found the greatest spiritual treasure.

May I become at all times, both now and forever
A protector for those without protection
A guide for those who have lost their way
A ship for those with oceans to cross
A bridge for those with rivers to cross
A sanctuary for those in danger
A lamp for those without light
A place of refuge for those who lack shelter
And a servant to all in need.

Anonymous

How little we realize the great importance of intercessory prayer. If at this moment you pray for someone, even though they are on the other side of the globe, the Lord Jesus will touch them.

Corrie ten Boom

The greatest thing anyone can do for God and others is pray. It is not the only thing; but it is the chief thing. The great people of the earth today are the people that pray. I do not mean those that talk about prayer; nor those who say they believe in prayer; nor yet those who can explain about prayer; but I mean those people who take time to pray.

S.D. Gordon

Prayer

We are not engaged in creating or producing anything, but in becoming aware of what is already the fact, namely that God is immediately and intimately present both to ourselves and to the ones for whom we are praying. Our task is to hold the awareness of this fact in the still centre of our being, to unite our love for them with God's love, in the quiet but total confidence that he will use our love to bring about the good in them which we both desire.

John Austin Baker

We understand very little about the power of prayer, and it is possible to misuse it even with the highest motives. I think I can only ask that God's will be done in regard to any situation and that people whom I want to help may come and seek him and know his love and truth directly. By the very act of asking, if I do it sincerely and without reserve, I open myself as a channel for God's healing action.

Elizabeth Gray Vining

To open oneself to another unconditionally in love is to be with him in the presence of God, and that is the heart of intercession. To pray for another is to expose both oneself and him to the common ground of our being: it is to see one's concern for him in terms of ultimate concern, to let God into the relationship. Intercession is to be with another at that depth, whether in silence or compassion or action.

John Robinson

O Lord, the help of the helpless,
The hope of the hopeless,
The Saviour of the storm-tossed,
The harbour of voyagers,
The physician of the sick;
We pray to you.

O Lord, you know each of us and our petitions,
You know each house and its needs;
Receive us all into your kingdom,
Make us children of light,
And bestow your peace and love upon us.

St Basil

৪০ ৪৩ ৪০

We can come to recognize as we pray for God's action on behalf of others that he wants to use us for the fulfilling of his purposes. What better picture of grace is there than this ... [the Spirit] deigns to use us and to make us valuable members of his body to effect his will on earth. In his perfection he hears our cry and comes to comfort us, to give us guidance, and to instruct us in ways we can serve his purposes.

Marva J. Dawn

Prayer

I used to ask God to help me. Then I asked if I might help him. I ended up by asking him to do his work through me.

James Hudson

ౠ ೞ ౠ

No form of prayer is more challenging than intercession, the prayer in which we ask God to grant our deepest desires, and it brings us closest to God as a Father. We ask for help in the belief that there is someone to hear us. But to ask for God's help is to go a step further. It is to believe that God loves us enough to respond – why should God answer our prayers if he does not love us and love us unconditionally? Why should our daily problems and hopes be of interest to God if he is not our Father in the truest sense of the word?

Cormac Murphy O'Connor

ౠ ೞ ౠ

I will not say that I will pray for you, but I shall think of you and God together.

George Macdonald

Praying as powerlessness

Andrew Clitherow

Generally speaking, human beings have strong natural drives towards self-preservation. They achieve security through the acquisition, preservation and accumulation of resources that are deemed necessary for survival in an environment that can at one and the same time be both life-enhancing and life-denying.

Against this background the broad structures of capitalist society meet our inner craving for security. Here competition and the survival of the fittest are justified by economic necessity. In the past there have been heroic attempts by some to find a social order that provides a deeper basis for social harmony than the survival of the fittest, where the poor exist almost by the permission of the rich. The sad reality seems to be that it is almost impossible to deny our inherited basic instincts – once used with good effect by our hunter-gatherer ancestors – in our pursuit of the need to secure a good income, housing, education and maybe even some kind of pension at the end.

Human nature, therefore, naturally equates power with success. The degree of power we have over where and how we work and live is usually determined by how successful we have become in acquiring good financial resources. The amount of power we have to influence others usually depends on how successful we have been in getting on and earning a good income.

Is there anything wrong with this, we might ask? Surely capitalism and Christianity are not mutually exclusive? At the end of the day, all we want to do is survive as best we can. And if we work hard and become one of the winners in the capitalist game, why should we not enjoy the prizes that await us? After all, much of the tax we pay is used for the benefit of others and we donate huge sums of money to charitable causes each year.

The problem with this, however, is that in such a culture of success the worth of individuals is measured either by their productivity (the work skills they can offer) or by their purchasing power as consumers. Moreover, as soon as financial transactions figure prominently in human relationships, love is often the first casualty.

Those of good faith soon recognize this kind of materialism – now a dominant factor in our daily lives – when it is imported into our relationship with God. Here the powerlessness of the cross is lost amongst our imperious demands for God to prove himself to us and to make us successful and powerful in all that we do. Through the life of Jesus Christ we are warned that if divine love is going to be the basis of our relationships, we have to be constantly aware of the ways in which, by subtle means, we integrate the power games we play in our daily lives into the way we pray and worship God. We soon forget that divine love moves restlessly over godless perspectives, as its values are not based on what we long to acquire and hold on to but on what we are prepared to give away and let go.

So do we need to feel guilty because of the many benefits we enjoy in our money-driven society? Certainly not. But we need to be extremely careful how we understand their significance if they are not to corrupt our relationship with God. To begin to pray in a way that places divine love in the heart of a pretty godless, consumer-driven, materialistic society means that we are bound to take up a counter-cultural stance. This will put us at odds with those who adopt an uncritical approach to the capitalist society and also those within churches that, to a greater or lesser degree, have sold out to a capitalist and consumerist approach to prayer.

The prayer by which we are united with God and begin to share in his divinity is neither vain nor even self-conscious. It doesn't deal in purchasing power or marketing. Nor is there any room for a throw-away attitude when prayer doesn't continue to delight. Authentic prayer, therefore, is devoid of much of what we count as essential for our happiness and security. To unearth the treasures of this prayer, therefore, is to learn how to be naked in the presence of God and not to be ashamed.

Some of the marks of this kind of prayer are as follows:

- Prayer is an expression of a loving relationship between God and ourselves and we rejoice daily in the freedom of access to God that this gives us. It is not something we can earn by good deeds. Nor is it something we do in order to keep in with God and get to heaven.

- Prayer is based on honesty. It is not a means for God to manipulate us and we do not use it to try and coerce God into delivering our selfish dreams. Instead we seek to learn how to live according to and within his will. It is therefore an adventure where, led by the Spirit, we end up in unexpected places. Here God constantly surprises us by the love he calls us to share and the effect this has on others.

- Prayer is free of the need for constant revision, updating and remodelling. While we may use and develop different ways of praying throughout our lives, this is not the same as always demanding new spiritual stimuli to tantalize and excite our emotions. While it is likely to affect the quality of our lives, authentic prayer is essentially not about a kind of spiritual tourism designed to give us a break from reality. Instead, by remaining pretty much in the same place, we can be led constantly and ever deeper into a holistic understanding of the spiritual and physical dimensions of worldly existence. Here we perceive increasingly the creative Spirit of God who is in and through all things.

- Prayer is founded on a disciplined devotion that takes time. It is not something we can discard when we judge that it has lost any kind of useful purpose. When prayer does not function according to our delights and the demands of our daily lives, we cannot consign it to the wheelie bin designated for wholly unsatisfactory spirituality. If we do, our prayer life is likely to be comprised of so many fits and starts that our experience of divine love will grow hardly at all.

- Prayer brings God and human beings closer together. Its primary aim is to lead us into an ever-deepening relationship with Christ as we participate increasingly in the energies of creation. Here it becomes increasingly difficult to define the line we like to draw between divinity and humanity. It is the primary process by which one day we too will come to know that 'It is no longer I who live, but it is Christ who lives in me' (Galatians 2.20).

- This prayer that is uncontaminated by our power-filled agendas in the world is Christ-centred in its focus and cross-shaped in its proclamation. As I say, it is completely counter-cultural in a consumer-driven, materialistic society. It is not something that we can add on to our faith. Instead it is at the heart of the Christian life. We mistakenly believe that we have been called to be religious people, whereas our real vocation is to an authentic way of human being. It is surely by now clear that our most powerful witness to a society turned off by perpetual struggles for power and control is through the prayerfulness of our lives.

So the most important thing the Christian does is to learn how to pray in this powerless kind of way. For it is the source of divine love in creation. Indeed, the Christian life *is* prayer, and the lives of individual Christians are prayers in themselves. Here and nowhere else are we able to access both the salvation of our souls and the redemption of the world.

Praying as powerlessness

Lord,
By prayerful offering
and heartfelt loving
may earth and heaven,
flesh and spirit,
human and divine,
combine to create
a communion of life
and love that lasts
for ever. Amen.

Andrew Clitherow

How did our ascetics, fathers and teachers warm the spirit of prayer inwardly, and establish themselves firmly in prayer? Their great object was to make the heart burn unceasingly towards the Lord alone. God claims the heart because within it lies the source of life. Where the heart is, there is consciousness, attention, mind; there is the whole soul.

The Art of Prayer

Waiting on the Lord takes us to the heart of prayer. When we wait, we are reminded that God works according to his time, not our convenience. When we wait, we are placed in a position of humility. Waiting puts us in the right place before God, longing for him to hear us and respond.

Stephen Eyre

Prayer

As we open our hearts to the Spirit, we shall begin to know the joy of God, or the love and compassion of God, or maybe his grief, when we pray. Prayer will simply be thinking God's thoughts after him, letting him use our bodies as a temple of his Spirit – a temple filled with praise or intercession. When, in obedience to God, we hoist our sails and begin to worship, give thanks and pray, whatever our feelings may be, we shall frequently find the wind of the Spirit filling those limp sails, inspiring us in our fellowship with God.

David Watson

Lord, teach me to listen. The times are noisy and my ears are weary with the thousand raucous sounds which continuously assault them. Give me the spirit of the boy Samuel when he said to you, 'Speak, for your servant hears.' Let me hear you speaking in my heart. Let me get used to the sound of your voice, that its tones may be familiar when the sounds of the earth die away, and the only sound will be the music of your speaking.

A.W. Tozer

The privilege of prayer to me is one of the most cherished possessions, because faith and experience alike convince me that God himself sees and answers ... In the quiet of home, in the heat of life and strife ... speech with God is inestimable.

Wilfred Grenfell

Thou hast redeemed me,
And therefore with hallelujahs
Do I praise thy Name,
Recounting the ancient glories
Which thou createdst in my soul,
And confessing
That infinitely more is left unsaid.
O my God,
Sanctify me by thy Spirit,
Make me a temple of the Holy Ghost
A willing person in the day of thy power.

Thomas Traherne

꙰   ꙮ   ꙰

God is not restricted by his attributes or by the way we recognize him. He is more than the sum total of all our experiences. He is the God who is the same yesterday, today and forever – the wholly other with whom we have to do. God is not a static god but the God who is to be discovered actively involved in the newness of each day and each event. God cannot be contained in a predictable pattern; he will be met in new ways and in making all things new.

David Adam

Prayer

How can we worship in prayer? By first reflecting upon who God is and thanking him for the things he has revealed about himself. To worship in prayer is to allow our spirits to feast upon what God has revealed concerning his acts in the distant and recent past, and what he has told us about himself. Slowly, as we review these things in a spirit of thanksgiving and recognition, we can sense our spirits beginning to expand, to take in the broader reality of God's presence and being.

Gordon MacDonald

It is in solitude, in that lonely life alone with God, in profound recollection of soul, in forgetfulness of all created things, that God gives himself to the soul that thus gives itself whole and entire to him.

Charles de Foucauld

Prayer is the fertile soil in which the insight into our true self in God takes root and grows. As our true awareness grows, as we see through the eyes of the Person we are, we see with a new vision. We see the Presence of God in all that is. Each thing becomes a symbol of communion with God just by being the thing it is.

James Finley

Prayer and defiance

John Davies

Half-past nine on a calm winter's evening: the dimly lit chapel of a lakeside retreat house: at the end of a day in quiet seclusion, sheltered by the house and well satisfied by meals supplied by the nuns, the members of the Retreat gather for Compline, the last act of worship of the day. An opening prayer, a hymn, psalms; then, a one-verse Scripture reading from Jeremiah:

> You, O Lord, are in the midst of us, and we are called by your name. Do not forsake us, O Lord our God.[1]

Compline is the last of the traditional monastic Hours of Prayer, which cover the day from dawn to sunset. All these Hours have much the same pattern; each consists of psalms, hymns, a portion of Scripture and prayers. Throughout the year, there is a lot of variety, according to the seasons. But in all the Hours of the medieval order, this short Scripture reading at Compline is the one element which never changes. For 365 nights of the year, there is this one reading. It reminds us that God is with us, that we are what we are because of what God is, and that we can rely on him not to desert us. As we go off to sleep, this is our security.

But there is more in this text than at first meets the eye. Look at Jeremiah 14. Verse 9 is embedded in a flow of anxiety; it is a flower of trust in a wasteland of depression and insecurity. In Jeremiah's day, the people for whom this was written were in the midst of disaster and failure, of exile from home, of drought, of loss of comfort and security. And God seems powerless. God has become homeless, a nomad like themselves, wandering as a stranger among them. Yet they can still say, 'You, O Lord, are among us; you are our identity; we have your signature upon us; don't forsake us.' So this prayer can be more than an expression of an overflowing sense of well-being; it can also be a defiance of all that our environment and experience are telling us.

The old monks and nuns who chose this verse as the Compline Scripture reading were not strangers to insecurity. In their own time, they knew that they could be singled out for attack. In a village close to where I live, a thousand monks were slaughtered in one day, at a time before Christianity was firmly established in our islands. In the midst of slaughter and calamity, they could make this prayer a song of defiance. They knew that, to all appearances, God may be useless in a crisis.[2] This so often feels to be true for us. But we still make our claim upon this God. We celebrate God's presence, God's naming of us, God's claiming of us. That is why this verse from Jeremiah does not need to be changed according to the season. God is in the midst of us in the arrival of Emmanuel in the degrading conditions of the Bethlehem manger. God is in the midst of us in the isolation of the temptation in the desert, in the loneliness of Gethsemane, in the disaster of Calvary.

For Jesus on that Friday, God is the apparent deserter. 'My God, my God, why have you forsaken me?'[3] He speaks to the God who seems to be absent. He knows that there is a reason, but he has to ask what that reason is. And God is in the midst of us, in the security of Easter victory and ascension triumph. As we follow the gospel story through the year, this verse from Jeremiah can fit the character of each day. It can neatly tie in with the security which the day affirms; or it can defy the natural implication of the day's story of disaster or failure. In the Christian pilgrimage, affirmation and defiance belong together.

The Hebrew scriptures are full of this defiance – defiance of the meaning of events around them, defiance of the powerful enemy, defiance of God: 'Though the fig tree does not blossom, and no fruit is on the vines, though the produce of the olive fails, and the fields yield no food ... yet I will rejoice in the LORD, I will exult in the God of my salvation.'[4] 'Though war rise up against me, yet I will be confident.'[5] 'See, [God] will kill me, but I will defend my ways to his face.'[6] And in the Christian hymns: 'We praise you, O God; we acknowledge you as Lord' – over against all the trivial tyrannies and the punitive dictatorship of state or religion. 'Heaven and earth are full of your glory' – in spite of so much evidence to the contrary. This is copper-bottomed faith. It is the religious equivalent of 'Don't let the b*****s get you down.'

The twentieth-century Welsh poet David Jones put this defiance into the prayer of first-century pre-Christian Welsh peasants. They are oppressed by the burden of the occupation of their land by the colonial power of Rome. They pray to their familiar local female divinity, who knows them and who can stand up for them against the macho uniformity of a controlling bureaucracy:

> In the bland megalopolitan light,
> Where no shadow is by day or by night,
> Be our shadow.[7]

The power-systems of empire – economic or political or military or ecclesiastical – think that they are doing good to us when they seek to control, to codify, to unify. They graciously bless us by illuminating us with the inescapable shadowless light of the neon tube, which never need be switched off. But the divine is merciful. In Jones' poem, the divine is represented in the Bearer of the Eternal Word, Mary of Nazareth, a peasant girl, voteless and voiceless, shifted around by Rome's manipulators. She will be our shadow, because the Mother of God is on the side of the individual's diversity, and against humanity's imperial systems of control, which rely on compulsion and statistics, which enumerate people and treat them as human beef. The same prayer can be made directly to the maternal protection of God the Creator. This, too, is the subversive prayer of defiance. God, be shadow for us. Mary, pray for us.

For the Hebrew people, the sign of their identity was the River Jordan. Jordan was the boundary that had to be crossed for entry into the Promised Land. Spiritually, it had to be recrossed in each generation and by each person. The freedom of the Promised Land had to be renewed again and again; otherwise, the people lost their sense of the land being a gift, and could behave as if it was theirs to grasp and occupy as outright owners. They often ignored their tenancy agreement with God; and prophets had to arise to defy the conventions, and to reassert the meaning of Jordan.

So 'Jordan' has come down to us as a symbol, with a massive wealth of meaning. Jordan is the physical river, muddy and unprepossessing; in it, our Lord was baptized as the mark of his subversive commitment to God's kingdom amid the world's authorities. Jordan is the political boundary, used by a community to define itself. It remains so, a sign of centuries of dispute and bloodshed. Pray for the peace of Jerusalem.

'Jordan' has become the symbol of the boundary that we cross at death. 'When I tread the verge of Jordan ...'. For me, this may not be far off. I await it with great interest; and part of me does not want the crossing to be delayed – there is so much to discover on the far side.

> Deep river, my home is over Jordan.
> Deep river, Lord.
> I want to cross over into campground, Lord.

Yes, I can make that prayer my own.

The first singers of 'Deep river' were black slaves, communicating with each other on the 'underground railroad' about their hope for freedom. The 'spirituals' they sang were highly political. They were songs of defiance, sung by people who knew that their status as slaves was not the final truth about themselves. For these singers, the 'Deep River Jordan' was the Ohio, the boundary between the slave states and the free. The song bundles together all the hopes and defiances of our calling. If I am interested in the 'spiritual' message about Jordan, I am also committed to the demand which it represents for justice and community among the children of God in this tortured world. My prayer for going home is also my defiance of the power-systems which try to tell me who I am. I am marked by the signature of God, and he will not forsake me.

Notes

1. Jeremiah 14.9.
2. See Rowan Williams, *Writing in the Dust: Reflections on 11th September and its Aftermath* (London, Hodder & Stoughton 2002), p. 8.
3. Mark 15.34.
4. Habakkuk 3.17-18.
5. Psalm 27.3.
6. Job 13.15.
7. David Jones, 'The Tutelar of the Place', quoted in *Poetry Wales*, Winter 1972, Llandbybie, Christopher Davies 1972, p. 44.

Be present, O merciful God,
and protect us through the silent hours of this
    night,
so that we who are wearied
by the changes and chances of this fleeting world,
may repose upon thy eternal changelessness;
through Jesus Christ our Lord.

Prayer from Compline

༄ ༄ ༄

As the day comes to its close and you are composing your
mind for sleep, run back over the day with your Lord. Yes!
With him. Remember, the aim is everything together. And you
are still together as you pass the day in review.

William Sangster

༄ ༄ ༄

The dawn is not distant,
Nor is the light starless;
Love is eternal!
God is still God, and
His faith shall not fail us –
Christ is eternal!

Anonymous

Prayer

I talk to [God] as a companion in prayer and praise, and our communion is delightful. He answers me again and again, often in words so clearly spoken that it seems my outer ear must have carried the tone, but generally in strong mental impressions. Usually a text of Scripture, unfolding some new view of him and his love for me, and care for my safety. That he is mine and I am his never leaves me, it is an abiding joy. Without it life would be a blank, a desert, a shoreless, trackless waste.

William James

Night is drawing nigh –
For all that has been – Thanks!
For all that shall be – Yes!

Dag Hammarskjöld

Anyone can sing in the sunshine. You and I should sing on when the sun has gone down, or when clouds pour out their rain, for Christ is with us.

Anonymous

The analogy I like best of God's upholding is that of the singer and the song. The song depends totally on being uttered by the singer, moment by moment. So it is, I believe, with God and the universe, including humankind. We owe our moment-by-moment existence to the upholding of God.

Colin Humphreys

୫୦ ୧୫ ୫୦

Be the peace of the Spirit mine this night
Be the peace of the Son mine this night
The peace of all peace be mine this night,
Each morning and evening of my life.

Celtic prayer

୫୦ ୧୫ ୫୦

The basic mistake which so many people make about prayer is that almost instinctively they regard prayer as a means of escape from a situation; and prayer is not primarily a means of escape, it is a means of conquest. The laws of life are not relaxed for us by prayer, but through prayer there comes the strength and power to endure and to overcome any situation.

William Barclay

Prayer

God of the ages, by whose hand
Through years long past our lives were led,
Give us new courage now to stand,
New faith to find the paths ahead.

Thou art the thought beyond all thought,
The gift beyond our utmost prayer;
No farthest reach where thou art not,
No height but we may find thee there.

Forgive our wavering trust in thee,
Our wild alarms, our trembling fears;
In thy strong hand eternally
Rests the unfolding of the years.

Though there be dark, uncharted space,
With worlds on worlds beyond our sight,
Still may we trust thy love and grace,
And wait thy word, 'Let there be light.'

Elisabeth Burrowes

Last words and prayers

John Lampard

The section 'Famous Last Words' is always a popular and sometimes amusing part of any dictionary of quotations. Among my favourites are the words of General Sedgwick who boasted, on seeing the enemy, 'They couldn't hit an elephant at this distance'; or the final words of Oscar Wilde, who hated the wallpaper in his bedroom, 'One of us must go'; and the words of the gravely ill Henrik Ibsen who, on hearing the nurse say that he was a little better, replied as his final words, 'On the contrary'.

A number of Christians have died with more noble words on their lips. Joseph Addison, the great hymn-writer, said, 'See in what peace a Christian can die.' Charles Frohman, who died at sea, said, 'Why fear death? It is the most beautiful adventure in life.' And (almost) the final words of John Wesley, the founder of Methodism, were, 'The best of all is God is with us' before he tried to repeat a hymn and then said, 'Farewell.' These famous final words were reproduced on pottery wall plaques and many a Methodist teapot.

It is not my purpose to invite you to say what your favourite 'Last Words' might be, amusing or spiritual, but to consider what are the last words you would like to hear said to you at the moment of death. What prayers or words would best feed and support your soul in your dying moments? This is not a morbid exercise, although the suggestion might shock you slightly.

One of the great traditions of the Christian Church can be found in a type of book called an *Ars Moriendi* (the Art of Dying). The art of dying, which was set out in these books, is to learn how to die a good death. At the heart of the *Ars Moriendi* was the conviction that thoughts about dying and death should not be left to the last minute. So you may be feeling fit and well, hoping to live many more years. Excellent: you are in the best possible state to think about the last words or prayers which will help you to have a good death. Part of the joy and wonder of a Christian's life is that, however mysterious and unknowable the future may be, we believe that we die into the fullness of Christ. Probably most Christians have doubts and fears at times in their lives about what lies beyond death, but the right prayers can help even the biggest doubter that there is more, in Christ.

In the oldest tradition of the Church, when a person was dying, the priest was instructed to read one of the gospel accounts of the passion narrative, so that the dying person, in his or her agony, was at one with their Lord in his agony from Gethsemane to the cross. This tradition was largely later replaced in the eighth century by the great prayer, 'Go forth, Christian soul', a very much shortened version of which can be found in the *Methodist Worship Book* (p. 431):

Go forth upon your journey, Christian soul,
in the name of God the Father who created you;
in the name of Jesus Christ who suffered for you;
in the name of the Holy Spirit who strengthens
    you;
in communion with the blessèd saints,
with angels and archangels
and with all the heavenly host.
May you rest in peace and may the City of God
be your eternal dwelling. Amen.

In the twentieth century these words, associated with dying, were included in some service books as part of the later funeral service, and you may have heard them said on such an occasion. These are the final words I most want to hear, but what would you like to hear said to you?

You might like to read through the following passages (and 'Go forth, Christian soul') imagining your final hours. You may surprise yourself that this is a comforting and spiritually supportive thing to do, and not something to be put off or shunned.

Some people will always vote for the 23rd Psalm, 'The Lord is my shepherd.' Although it is a psalm rather than a prayer, the two categories come together in these evocative words. There are many fine modern biblical versions of it, and excellent hymn versions (the hymn tune Crimond is often used as a means of referring to the 23rd Psalm) but this is the traditional version from the 1611 Bible:

The LORD *is* my shepherd; I shall not want.
He maketh me to lie down in green pastures: he leadeth me
beside the still waters.
He restoreth my soul: he leadeth me in the paths of righteousness
for his name's sake.
Yea, though I walk through the valley of the shadow of death, I will
fear no evil: for thou *art* with me; thy rod and thy staff they comfort me.
Thou preparest a table before me in the presence of mine enemies:
thou anointest my head with oil; my cup runneth over.
Surely goodness and mercy shall follow me all the days of my life:
and I will dwell in the house of the LORD for ever.

Other people, and I am among them, are also attracted to the words of the *Nunc Dimittis* (the Latin for 'Now dismiss'). These are the words spoken by the old man Simeon who worshipped in the Jerusalem Temple. He had longed during the whole of his life of devotion that, before he died, he would have the privilege of seeing the longed-for Messiah. When Mary and Joseph brought the Christ-child to the Temple Simeon took him in his arms and blessed God. He then spoke these familiar words (again from the 1611 Bible):

> Lord, now lettest thou thy servant depart in peace, according to thy word:
> for mine eyes have seen thy salvation,
> which thou hast prepared before the face of all people;
> A light to lighten the Gentiles, and the glory of thy people Israel.

Our own experience will never be as dramatic as that of Simeon, with the opportunity to hold the Christ-child in our arms, but in our different ways we can each reflect that our Christian lives echo the words 'mine eyes have seen thy salvation'.

Many people's spiritual sustenance comes through the words of well-loved hymns from our hymn books. We have already seen that John Wesley tried to say the words of a hymn as he was dying. You might like to consider if there are any hymns you would like said or sung as you are dying. Here are a few suggestions, but you will do better thinking about your own favourites.

'O thou who camest from above', especially the last verse, 'Till death thy endless mercies seal/and make the sacrifice complete'; or 'The day thou gavest, Lord, is ended'; or 'This, this is the God we adore ....We'll praise him for all that is past, and trust him for all that's to come.'

My final words are these. When you have made your choice, make sure that those you love know what they are so, if at the last you cannot tell them, they can share with you *your* choice of final words.

Prayer

O Lord, whose way is perfect:
Help us, we pray,
Always to trust in your goodness
That, walking with you in faith
And following you in all simplicity,
We may possess quiet and contented minds,
And cast all our care on you;
For the sake of Jesus Christ our Lord.

Christina Rossetti

ԑ℧   ℭ℥   ԑ℧

For what is it to die but to stand naked in the wind
    and to melt into the sun?
And what is it to cease breathing but to free the
    breath from its restless tides,
that it may rise and expand and seek God
    unencumbered?

Only when you drink from the river of silence shall
    you indeed sing.
And when you have reached the mountain top,
    then you shall begin to climb.
And when the earth shall claim your limbs, then
    you shall truly dance.

Kahlil Gibran

Last words and prayers

Trust the past to God's mercy, the present to God's love and the future to God's providence.

Augustine

As a boat is tossed by the storm,
So my trust in you, God, is wavering.
I have prayed for healing,
Cried to you for a miracle,
But am still left suffering.
My confidence in you is shaken.
Can it be that in my vulnerability
You will come to be with me?
Living Jesus, transform my brokenness
So death may be the gateway to new life.
Your faithful love is sufficient,
So I rest in you.

Ann Shepherdson

Prayer that runs its course till the last day of life needs a strong and tranquil soul.

Clement of Alexandria

Prayer

Stay with us, Lord, the day is travelled far;
we meet thee at its close.
Lord, at our humble table sit and share,
and be our sweet repose.

Pledge of our hospitality, the bread
is broken by thy hands;
our quaking love, our most confiding dread
beholds and understands.

We cannot be without thee, Lord, because
the night is perilous;
and anxiously our earthly journey draws
to evening, stay with us.

John Henry Gray

 howe cg howe

Our valleys may be filled with foes and
tears; but we can lift our eyes to the
hills to see God and the angels,
heaven's spectators, who support us
according to God's infinite wisdom as
they prepare our welcome home.

Billy Graham

Prayer is
The world in tune,
A spirit voice,
And vocal joys,
Whose echo is heaven's bliss.

Henry Vaughan

Nothing can separate you from God's love, absolutely nothing. God is enough for time, God is enough for eternity. God is enough!

Hannah Whitall Smith

O Lord, the first and the last,
the beginning and the end;
you who were with us at our birth,
be with us through our life,
be with us at our death;
and because your mercy will not leave us then,
grant that we die not,
but rise to the life everlasting.

The Cambridge Bede Book

Contributors

Liz Babbs is an award-winning author, performer, broadcaster and spiritual mentor. A former ME sufferer, and Patron of the charity Hope for ME, she travels extensively raising awareness of health and spirituality issues. She is the author of nine books and two CDs, including *Into God's Presence – Listening to God through prayer and meditation* (Zondervan 2005). She has led workshops on relaxation and meditation at major conferences, festivals and retreat centres. For more information contact www.lizbabbs.com

Andrew Clitherow is Director of Training for the Diocese of Blackburn and a Canon Residentiary of Blackburn Cathedral. He is the author of *Into Your Hands: Prayer, and the Call to Holiness in Everyday Ministry and Life* (SPCK 2001) and *Renewing Faith in Ordained Ministry: New Hope for Tired Clergy* (SPCK 2004).

Frank Collier has spent much of his professional life in teaching Religious Education and has been an active Methodist local preacher for over 60 years. He has written a number of Bible study series, published by Foundery Press, initially for his local house groups at Rhos-on-Sea Methodist Church in Colwyn Bay, but now used by people of many different denominations.

139

Prayer

John Davies was Church of England Bishop of Shrewsbury 1987-94. Previously he was for many years a priest in rural parishes and city university ministry in South Africa, Wales and England. He was also Principal of the College of Ascension, Selly Oak, and a Canon of St Asaph Cathedral, and has written several books and study guides on biblical themes. John Davies and his wife now live very close to the Welsh/English border, and are associate members of the Iona Community.

Robert Dolman read History and Theology at Emmanuel College, Cambridge, and after a time spent teaching he studied at Queen's College, Birmingham and was ordained as a Methodist presbyter in 1976. He has served in various Methodist circuits, in two student chaplaincies and three Local Ecumenical Partnerships. In 2000 he gave the Fernley Hartley Lecture at the Methodist Conference on the poet George Herbert, and his interests include the interplay between religion, literature and the arts and politics.

Deborah Smith Douglas is an American Episcopalian laywoman who has travelled extensively in Britain, and with her family spent two sabbatical years in St Andrews. She has degrees in literature and law, and is trained in spiritual direction. She gives retreats across the United States and in Scotland and England, and writes essays and articles for a variety of Christian periodicals. A Benedictine oblate, she is the author of *The Praying Life: Seeking God in All Things*

(Continuum 2003) and, with her husband David Douglas, co-author of *Pilgrims in the Kingdom: Travel in Christian Britain* (BRF 2005).

Geoffrey Duncan has compiled a number of worship anthologies, including *Shine On Star of Bethlehem, Entertaining Angels, Let Justice Roll Down* and *Harvest for the World* for Christian Aid. These are all published by the Canterbury Press.

Rod Garner is an Anglican priest in Southport and Theological Consultant to the Diocese of Liverpool. He has extensive experience of urban ministry and a research interest in the contemporary city. He is the author of *Facing the City: Urban Mission in the 21st Century* (Epworth 2004) and *Like a Bottle in the Smoke* (Inspire 2006).

Lorna Lackenby is currently training as a local preacher in the Methodist Church and is enjoying being able to take a creative approach to worship. She has always had an interest in the arts and is involved in leading a Christian Dance Club. She has taken part in leading workshops involving writing, craft, art and dance and finds it a privilege to encourage others to worship in new and creative ways. She has recently married Mark, whom she met at her local church, where they were married.

John Lampard is a retired Methodist minister living in Walthamstow, a multi-cultural borough in London. For nine years he was Local Preachers' Secretary for the Methodist Church, and was also responsible for introducing its *Faith & Worship* training course. He is the author of *Go forth, Christian Soul: The biography of a prayer* (Epworth 2006). In retirement he is overseeing the building of a new church in Hackney, and the fruitful development of an allotment.

Ann Lewin is a well-known writer and retreat leader. She is the author of a number of books of poetry, the latest of which is *Watching for the Kingfisher* (Inspire 2004). She has also written *Words by the Way* (Inspire 2005), a collection of ideas and worship resources for a wide range of occasions throughout the Christian year. Ann Lewin's next book, *Growing in Love: through Lent with Julian of Norwich* will be published by Inspire in November 2006.

Pam Pointer is a freelance writer and speaker whose work reflects her interest in the study of society and of the value, role and relationship of individuals within it. Pam lived and worked in London for many years before moving to Wiltshire. She is the author of several books, writes features and columns for various publications, and broadcasts Morning Thoughts for BBC Radio Wiltshire.

Contributors

John Pritchard has been the Bishop of Jarrow since 2002. He studied Theology at Cambridge and in 1980 became vicar of a large parish in Taunton. He became Director of Pastoral Studies at Cranmer Hall, Durham, where he became Warden in 1993. In 1996 he moved to become Archdeacon of Canterbury and Canon Residentiary of Canterbury Cathedral. He has written numerous books, including *The Intercessions Handbook* (1997), *How to Pray* (2002) and *Living Easter through the Year* (2005). His hobbies include fell-walking, photography, travel and reading.

Jackie Stead is the editor of *Woman Alive*, the magazine for today's Christian woman, and also *Women of the Word*, a collection of studies on women in the Bible from the magazine published by BRF. She was previously features editor for *Christian Herald*.

Yvonne Walker is Chair of the Methodist Retreat and Spirituality Network. She gives retreats, quiet days, workshops and spiritual direction. For many years she was UK Convener of the Julian Meetings.

Acknowledgements

Inspire gratefully acknowledges the use of copyright items. Every effort has been made to trace copyright owners, but where we have been unsuccessful we would welcome information which would enable us to make appropriate acknowledgement in any reprint.

Scripture quotations are from the New Revised Standard Version of the Bible, (Anglicized Edition) © 1989, 1995 by the Division of Christian Education of the National Council of Churches of Christ in the United States of America. Used by permission. All rights reserved.

Page

12   John Main, *Word into Silence*, Darton, Longman and Todd.

20   *New Every Morning*, BBC 1983.

20   John Macquarrie, *Paths in Spirituality*, SCM Press 1972.

20   Frederick Wilcox, *The Lord's Prayer for Today*, Epworth Press 1950.

21   Michael Ramsay, *Be Still and Know*, Fount 1982.

22   Frank Collier, *The Lord's Prayer*, Foundery Press 1994.

23   Peter Doble, *The Disciples' Prayer*, Foundery Press 2000.

23 Stephen Cottrell, *Praying through Life*, Church House Publishing 2003.

29 Sally Magnusson, *Glorious Things*, Continuum 2004.

30 Pat Robson, *The Celtic Heart*, Fount 1998. By permission of the author.

31 Anne Treneer, *Schoolhouse in the Wind*, Exeter University Press 1998.

32 Amy Carmichael, *Golden Cord*, Christian Literature Crusade. Permission applied for.

40 Walter Wangerin, *The Book of God*, Lion Publishing 1996.

40 Donald Soper, *It is Hard to Work for God*, Epworth Press 1957.

41 Carlo Carretto, *The God Who Comes*, Darton, Longman and Todd 1981.

41 James Jones, *People of the Blessing*, Bible Reading Fellowship 1998.

47 Pat Marsh, 'Silent Strength', *Silent Strength*, Inspire 2005.

47 Mother Teresa, in Malcolm Muggeridge, *Something Beautiful for God*, HarperCollins 1971.

48 Andrew Knowles, *Discovering Prayer*, Lion Publishing 1985.

49   Robert Van de Weyer, *Celtic Parables*, SPCK 1997. Permission applied for.

49   Dorothy Day, 'Room for Christ', *The Catholic Worker* 1945.

62   J.B. Phillips, *New Testament Christianity*, Fount 1962.

71   Evelyn Underhill, *Worship*, Eagle 1991.

72   Donald Coggan, *The People's Bible Commentary: Psalms 1-72*, Bible Reading Fellowship 1998.

72   John Drane, *Introducing the Old Testament*, Lion Publishing 1987.

73   Cyril Skerratt, *Exploring Prayer*, Methodist Publishing House 1993.

73   Adrian Curtis, *Psalms*, Epworth Commentaries, Epworth 2004.

74   Rita Snowden, *Sung in our Hearts*, Epworth Press 1952.

74   Stephen B. Dawes, *Prayer*, Thinking Things Through, Epworth Press 2003.

80   'Harvest', *Seasonal Worship in the Countryside*, The Staffordshire Seven, SPCK 2003. Permission applied for.

80   Esther de Waal, *The Celtic Way of Prayer*, Hodder & Stoughton 1996.

80   Ray Buckley, 'From our hands: the creator and real people' in *Magnet: Creative Spirit*, Autumn 2003.

81   Morton T. Kelsey, *The Other Side of Silence*, SPCK 1977.

82 Edmund Banyard, *Turn but a Stone*, NCEC. Permission applied for.

83 Bruce Milne, *Know the Truth*, IVP 1982.

88 C.S. Lewis, *Letters to an American Lady*, Eerdman's 1975.

88 Peter Marshall, *Mr Jones, Meet the Master*, Fleming H. Revell/Peter Davies Ltd.

89 Malcolm Spencer, (adapted) in Leslie Weatherhead, *A Private House of Prayer*, Hodder & Stoughton 1961.

90 Elizabeth Goudge, *Green Dolphin Country*, Hodder & Stoughton 1944.

90 Michel Quoist, *Prayers of Life*, Gill and Macmillan 1963.

96 Philip J. Fisher, *Prayers out of Church*, Epworth Press 1958.

97 Edward Wilson in George Seaver, *Edward Wilson of the Antarctic*, John Murray 1935.

99 David N. Francis, *About Prayer*, Epworth Press 1957.

106 John Austin Baker, *The Foolishness of God*, Darton Longman and Todd 1970.

106 John Robinson, *Honest to God*, SCM 1963.

107 Marva J. Dawn, *To Walk and not Faint*, Eerdmans 1997.

108 Cormac Murphy O'Connor, *Old in Years and Young in Soul*, ed. Keith Albans, Methodist Homes for the Aged 2003.

Prayer

115 Stephen Eyre, *Time with God*, IVP 1995.

116 David Watson, *Discipleship*, Hodder & Stoughton 1983.

117 David Adam, *Forward to Freedom*, Darton, Longman and Todd 1999.

118 Gordon MacDonald, *Ordering Your Private World*, Highland Books 1987.

118 James Finley, *Merton's Palace of Nowhere*, Ave Maria Press 1978.

127 Colin Humphreys, in Jean Watson, *The Spirit of Peace*, Lion Publishing 1994.

127 William Barclay, *The Plain Man's Book of Prayers*, Fontana 1959.

128 Elisabeth Burrowes, © 1958 The Hymn Society/Hope Publishing Company. Administered by CopyCare, PO Box 77, Hailsham BN27 3EF, music@copycare.com

135 Ann Shepherdson, in *Old in Years and Young in Soul*, ed. Keith Albans, Methodist Homes for the Aged 2003. Permission applied for.

148